Meditation: How To Reduce Stress, Get Healthy, And Find Your Happiness In Just 15 Minutes A Day

By Rachel Rofe'
http://www.YourBestMeditation.com

All rights reserved. No portion of this ebook may be reproduced or transmitted in any form whatsoever, electronic or mechanical, including email, forums, photocopying, recording, or by any informational storage or retrieval system without the express written, dated and signed permission of its authors.

This program contains material protected under International and Federal Copyright Laws and Treaties and may not be reprinted or distributed for any purpose.

© 2010 Rachel Rofe

DISCLAIMER

Yes, I know disclaimers aren't fun. But they're a necessity and this one is no different. For starters, I am not responsible for your actions or lack thereof. I have used my best efforts in preparing this book and make no representation or warranties with respect to its accuracy, applicability, or completeness. In real-speak: I don't know you, and I don't know your medical conditions. Hence, if anything seems uncomfortable to you, please ask your doctor first.

I, Rachel Rofe,, shall in no event be held liable for any loss or other damages, including but not limited to special, incidental, consequential, or other damages.

Table of Contents

Introduction: Discovering Everyday Meditation   14

Examining Meditation's Long History – and Its Myths   18

Discovering the History of Meditation   19

Debunking the Meditation Myths   23

Myth #1: You need to be able to twist yourself up like a pretzel.   25

Myth #2: Meditation is a religious experience.   26

Myth #3: Meditation is about letting your mind go blank. 28

Myth #4: Meditation results in crazy experiences.   30

Myth #5: Meditation is just self-hypnosis.   32

Myth #6: True meditation means sitting cross-legged and chanting "om." 34

Myth #7: Meditation is difficult. 34

Reflect 36

Reaping the Many Benefits of Meditation 37

Physical Benefits 39

Emotional and Psychological Benefits 50

Spiritual Benefits 60

Reflect 67

Choosing the Best Meditation Technique 69

Distinguishing Between the Two Main Types of Meditation 69

Concentration (Structured) Meditation 70

Mindfulness (Unstructured) Meditation 74

1) Activity Meditation 77

2) Concept Meditation 82

3) Yoni Mudra Meditation 86

4) Basic Breath Meditation 89

5) Death Meditation 93

6) Energy Meditation 97

7) Dualistic Meditation 99

8) Transcendental MeditationTM 102

9) Mantra Meditation 104

10) Body Scan Meditation 107

11) Eating Meditation 111

12) Writing Meditation   112

13) Chakra Meditation   117

14) Zen Meditation 121

Reflect, Plus Which Type of Meditation is Right for You?   128

Getting Started: The Basics of Simple Meditation   130

Approaching Meditation: Attitude and Mindset 130

Motivating Yourself to Meditate   151

Tip #1: Make a list of your reasons for meditation.   155

Tip #2: Stop yourself when you make excuses.   157

Tip #3: Keep a meditation journal.   160

Tip #4: Create a ritual.   163

Tip #5: Just do it.   165

Tip #6: Meditate for short periods.   167

Tip #7: Try activity meditation.   168

Tip #8: Use tools like guided meditation scripts (recording).   170

Tip #9: Find someone to hold you accountable.   171

Reflect   175

Preparing to Meditate   177

Setting Aside Time to Meditate   177

Selecting a Quiet Place to Meditate   184

Creating the Mood   189

Choosing Comfortable Clothing 191
Reflect 196

Learning the Basics of Meditation 197
Choosing Your Position 197
Sitting Positions 199
Lying Positions 208
Standing Positions 213
Activity Positions 215
Breathing Correctly: The Power of Breath 217
How Do You Breathe? 220
Breath Awareness 227
Breathing with Your Diaphragm 228
Becoming Aware of Your Breath 231
Advanced Breath Awareness 238
Learning Breathing Techniques 243
Weighted-Abdomen Breathing Technique 244
Alternate Nostril Breathing Technique 245
Walking Breath 250
"The Bee" Technique 252

Ujjayi Breathing Technique 253
Skull Shining Breath Technique 254
Breath-Slowing Technique 255
Breath-Mantra Meditation 258
Reflect 260

Focusing Your Mind 261
Tamping Down the Perfectionist 267
Strengthening Your "Focus Muscle" 274
Reflect 282

Handling Unexpected Body Sensations and Other Feelings 284

Dealing with Unexpected Body Sensations 284
Handling Pain 286
Handling Other Sensations During (and After) Meditation 288
Physical Sensations 290
"Energy" Sensations 302
Dealing With Unexpected Feelings 311

Handling Unpleasant Feelings 311

Opening Your Heart to Unconditional Love and Forgiveness 316

Love and Forgiveness Meditation 321

Dealing With Other Unexpected Feelings 324

Enjoying Pleasant Feelings 332

Reflect 340

Incorporating Meditation Into Your Everyday Life 342

Fitting Meditation Into Your Life 342

Choosing a Practice That Suits You 349

Structured vs. Unstructured? 350

Guided Meditation vs. Self Meditation?   352

Reflect   358

Enhancing Your Meditation Sessions   361

Meditation Clothing   364

Meditation Timers   365

Meditation Stools, Mats, Pillows   367

Mood-Setting and Other Meditation Tools   370

Guided Meditation Recordings and Scripts   373

Advanced Meditation Resources   375

Conclusion: Taking the Next Step on Your Journey...   377

Introduction: Discovering Everyday Meditation

Just say the word "meditation" to most folks, and they'll conjure up an image of people sitting cross-legged, chanting mantras and contemplating life. Or maybe they'll imagine Buddhist monks in long robes, dutifully meditating to get closer to their god.

Ommmmm… (You can almost hear them chanting, right?)

What you don't imagine is a professional man (with the high-stress job) stretched back in his favorite recliner meditating. And you don't imagine the single mom who gets someone else to watch the kids for a few minutes so she can meditate. Yet these are the folks who can benefit the most from meditation.

And these are people just like you.

That's why I created this book. You see, I'm not a yogi. I haven't devoted my life to meditation. I don't sit around on mountaintops doling out wisdom or leading people to their bliss.

Instead, I teach everyday people – people just like you – how to reap the benefits of simple meditation in as little as 15 minutes per day.

I'm not going to tell you to seek out a guru (unless you want one) and I'm not going to tell you to go on a pilgrimage to a far off place (unless you want to).

Just stick with me, and you'll learn everyday meditation from an everyday kind of person.

Here's just a small sample of what you'll discover inside this book:

- You'll discover what meditation really is – and you'll find out what's true and what's just a myth.

- You'll discover the physical, emotional and spiritual benefits of meditation.

- You'll find out the two main categories and ten subcategories of meditation. (And you'll learn which one is right for you.)

- You'll learn the quick and easy way to get started meditating as soon as today.
- You'll find out how to control your breath, thoughts, body and

your feelings like never before.

- You'll discover how to incorporate simple meditation into your everyday life.

- You'll get a list of tools you can use to enhance your enjoyment.

And much more.

Look, by the time you finish this book you won't be levitating or going into any death-like trances. But you will know the secrets of leading a healthier, happier life by incorporating meditation into your daily routine.

Let's get started...

Examining Meditation's Long History – and Its Myths

Before we rush into this subject, let's define meditation for our purposes:

Meditation is a relaxed state of awareness. It's a mind-control technique that results in you feeling calm and relaxed.

TIP: If you asked a yogi or a Buddhist monk for a definition, you'd get a slightly different one. That's because those who practice certain types of meditation do so almost purely for spiritual reasons. For example, monks may use it as part of a spiritual awakening. And so any definition they give you would include a spiritual component.

For our purposes, we're going to view meditation primarily in light of its emotion and physical benefits since that's something everyone can appreciate. And for those who'd like to take it a step further, you can reap the spiritual benefits as well.

Discovering the History of Meditation

It's hard to pinpoint the exact moment in history when

meditation started. We just know what people have been meditating for thousands of years.

Some experts suggest that ancient people first became aware of meditation as they stared into the dancing flames of their fires. The meal is over, people are relaxed. The kids fall asleep next to their parents. The conversation dies down and everyone stares into the fire, focusing on the flames dancing and leaping.

Thoughts of the day's hunt fade away. Thoughts of tomorrow's hunt don't even enter the mind of the person staring into the fire. His full focus is on a single flame.

He relaxes. He has no desire to pull his eyes from the flame. And suddenly he becomes much more aware of everything – his body, this thoughts, the greater world around him. He enjoys a relaxed state of awareness. And once he realizes what caused this awareness (putting forth 100% of his attention on the flame), he's able to replicate and teach the experience.

While the above is mere speculation, we do have recorded Indian scriptures (called tantras) that mention meditation techniques. These tantras date back 5000 years!

Around 500 B.C., one of the most well-known proponents of meditation entered the scene: Buddha. Buddha's teachings quickly spread across what is now the Asian continent, with different practitioners tweaking the techniques to suit their own preferences. Even today, the original Buddha-inspired meditation and its derivatives are some of the most popular forms of meditation.

It took a few thousand years for meditation to reach the West. Even after it arrived, it didn't immediately gain a foothold, perhaps due in large part to the myths surrounding meditation.

For example, many people in the U.S. believed that meditation created a state of catatonia. And since catatonia is typically associated with people who have schizophrenia or other mental illness, you can see the reluctance of people to pile onto the meditation bandwagon!

Eventually folks did come around and warm to the idea of meditation. By the 1960's and 1970's, respected people like college professors were talking about, researching, teaching and then praising meditation and its benefits.

Side Note: Incidentally, people in the U.S. came to appreciate the altered state of consciousness they could achieve through meditation right around the time they were appreciating the altered state of consciousness achieved with recreational drugs like marijuana. Coincidence?

From there, meditation continued to grow in popularity. Groups sprung up all around the Western world to help others teach and reap the benefits of meditation. And that brings us today, where the everyday person has now discovered how meditation can help bring about feelings of peace and a healthier body.

Debunking the Meditation Myths

I'll be honest: The myths surrounding meditation still exist.

If you don't believe it, just tell all your friends that you're going to start meditating. If all your friends are already enlightened about the benefits of meditation, then tell all your coworkers. Tell the guy next to you in line at the post office. Tell the cop who stops you for speeding.

Go ahead – tell as many people as you can and watch their reactions. You'll see eyebrows pop up like a child's Jack-in-the-box toy. You'll witness the smirking "Mona Lisa" smiles of those who're trying to keep a straight face. And you'll hear the laughs from those who think you've gone all "Twilight Zone" on them.

> *SIDE NOTE: Maybe you're not even completely sure about this whole meditation thing. Let me ask you this – Is this book sitting on your desktop so everyone who walks by*

your computer can see it? Or did you tuck it away into a folder so no one would see what you're reading? If you're feeling a little weird about even owning this book, then this next section is for you.

Forget about what everyone else thinks. Pat yourself on the back for doing something good for you. And then read these seven myths so that you know what to tell someone the next time they flash that smirky smile at you...

Myth #1: You need to be able to twist yourself up like a pretzel.

You've probably seen some people meditating in positions that made you think these folks must have legs made of rubber. Just *looking* at them sent shots of pain down your legs and made you wish you had a morphine drip hooked up. It's enough to turn you off from meditation forever.

Wait, hang on… come back!

Here's the thing: You don't need to sit in those sorts of unusual positions. Some people do. But then again, those people probably have been sitting like that since they were children. What looks painful to you is probably rather normal to them.

But that doesn't mean you have to sit like that to meditate. Not at all. If you want to recline back in your favorite Easy Chair, go ahead. If you want to sit on the floor, great. If you want to lie down, that's fine too. The choice is yours.

Myth #2: Meditation is a religious experience.

Because people like Buddha (and the Buddhist monks) popularized meditation, and because religious people who meditate do describe it as a religious experience, many people believe that you must be religious to meditate.

Not true.

Think of it this way...

Monks through the ages have popularized other activities, such as growing your own food in a vegetable garden. But that doesn't mean you need to be religious in order to be a gardener.

Same goes for meditation. You don't need to follow a certain religion (or even consider yourself religious in any way) in order to reap the physical and emotional benefits of meditation.

However, those who want to take it a step further can certainly enjoy the spiritual benefits of meditation. If you choose a type of meditation that encourages you to focus on a certain concept, you may want to focus on a spiritual or even religious concept (like forgiveness, unconditional love, the connectedness of all people and so on).

But by no means is this a requirement in order to enjoy the other physical and emotional benefits of meditation. An atheist can enjoy meditation just as much as devout followers of any religion.

Myth #3: Meditation is about letting your mind go blank.

Here are the mind myths. Most people think that meditation is all about letting your mind go blank. Or if you're not letting it go blank, then you're contemplating life.

First off, meditation is about controlling your thoughts.

Depending on what type of meditation you're practicing, you may seek to focus on a single thought (or an object) while letting all other thoughts fade away. Alternatively, you may let your mind wander, but you do so as an attached observer (rather than reacting to whatever you're thinking about).

The point is, your mind doesn't go blank. Instead, you learn to control whatever it is you're thinking about (or at least control your reaction). But you don't stop thinking. (That happens when you die. ☺)

Now the second myth is that people who meditate are just a bunch of "navel gazers" who're contemplating life. Instead of thinking about things like what to study in college or what type of job to apply for, these folks think about the big questions like, "Why am I here?" and "What is love?"

While it's true that there ARE some people who meditate on these types of questions, that doesn't mean you have to. Indeed, you don't have to meditate on any questions or concepts at all. So no, the desire to contemplate life's mysteries is NOT a requirement for those wanting to learn how to meditate.

Myth #4: Meditation results in crazy experiences.

Because meditation can induce an altered state of consciousness, many people immediately assume that it produces crazy experiences.

In order to deal with this myth, we probably need to define the word "crazy."

- If you think that the altered states of awareness you get when you're falling asleep or just waking up are crazy (such as that floating feeling), then maybe meditation is crazy.

- If you think the altered states you feel when you're deliriously tired or wide awake and energetic are crazy, then maybe meditation is a little crazy.

- If you think the altered states produced by caffeine, nicotine, alcohol and other light drugs are completely crazy, then yeah... maybe meditation does produce crazy experiences.

The point is, you experience altered states of consciousness every single day… without even trying! Right now as you read this you're in a totally different state of awareness than you were last night while you were sleeping.

Meditation is simply a means of deliberately controlling your natural internal states and your consciousness. And isn't that better than being controlled by your internal states?

Myth #5: Meditation is just self-hypnosis.

Meditation and self-hypnosis do share some common components, in that they both can produce altered states of consciousness and awareness. In addition, both cannot be achieved unless the person wants to be hypnotized or wants to meditate. And in fact, you may enter a hypnotic state in much the same way you enter a meditative state (by putting all your focus and attention on one object or concept).

However, hypnosis is usually used in therapy... and usually to treat something very specific. For example, it may be used to help someone remember something they've repressed, it may help them lose weight or perhaps they'll use hypnosis to calm an anxiety.

Meditation *can* be used as a therapy to treat special ailments. However, meditation is different because it can also be used simply to contribute to an overall feeling of calm and well being. As you'll soon see, there are many emotional, physical and spiritual benefits of meditation.

Myth #6: True meditation means sitting cross-legged and chanting "om."

Here's what we talked about in the beginning of this book. Specifically, how mentioning the word meditation brings up images of people in long robes, cross-legged, saying "om" and burning incense.

Do people like this exist? Of course – and you can do it too (if you want to). But you don't have to do that. You can get just as much benefit by sitting in your sweat pants and t-shirt... and never uttering the word "om."

Myth #7: Meditation is difficult.

You hear about people spending hours a day in meditation. Usually, these are the same people who've spent the last 30 or 40 years refining their technique. It's no wonder the average person thinks that meditation is difficult!

Listen, meditation is like anything else. Consider this…

You can learn how to play chess. Maybe you'll play it a few times per year. And every time you play, you find it incredibly enjoyable.

On the flip side, there are the chest masters who play every single day. What's more, they've been honing their chest skills for decades. They live it and breathe it. They've devoted their life to mastering it.

The same goes for meditation. Even if you don't immerse yourself in it, you can still enjoy it. And if you find you like it so much that you want to devote more time to it, you can do that too.

Reflect

You just learned about the long history of meditation that goes back thousands of years. You also discovered the truth about meditation as we examined some of the most common myths.

Now let's turn our attention to the benefits of meditation...

Reaping the Many Benefits of Meditation

If you think the main benefits of meditation include sitting on a mountaintop and wearing a funky robe, you haven't been paying attention! But read on, because you're about to discover in detail al the physical, emotional and spiritual benefits you'll get when you start meditating.

But let me throw in a disclaimer here...

You're not going to receive all these benefits immediately. It doesn't happen overnight. Indeed, it's a gradual process, where the more regularly you meditate, the more likely it is you'll notice and enjoy the associated benefits.

You can think of meditation in the same way you think about exercising. If you exercise for the first time ever today, you can't reasonably expect that your chances of having a heart attack drop to zero. You won't lose ten pounds from one exercise session. Nor can you expect to get into shape so fast that you're ready to run a marathon tomorrow.

However, you probably will sleep a little better tonight. You'll feel pretty good physically, and you'll even get that good feeling just because you're proud of yourself. You'll kick your metabolism up a notch for a few hours. You may feel more relaxed today.

The same goes for meditation. You'll feel good both during and after your session. But you'll only experience the best benefits if you commit to meditating regularly.

Now let's take a peek at some of these benefits. Please note that I'm not just throwing out theories about meditation. These benefits are backed up with scientific research. And once you start meditating, you'll experience them for yourself...

Physical Benefits

While people have used meditation for all sorts of reasons, in recent times there has been a surge of practitioners and fans who use it because of its physical benefits. And one of the main physical benefits you'll enjoy when you start meditating is a reduction in the signs and symptoms of stress.

Obviously, just the act of pulling yourself away from the chaos of life is going to help you manage stress. But meditation goes beyond that. That means you'll get more benefits if you use your "me time" to meditate as opposed to using it for some other activity (like napping or taking a bubble bath).

Here's why…

Scientists discovered that meditation actually affects your brain activity. The typical stressed-out person's brain has lot of activity in the frontal cortex (which is linked to anxiety and depression) as well as in the amygdala (which is where fear is processed).

But get this: When you meditate, the brain's frantic activity calms and moves to a different part of the brain (the left frontal cortex). And that means you're feeling calmer and less stressed out.

That's not all…

Have you heard of cortisol? This is a hormone your body releases when you're feeling stressed.

While you can certainly handle cortisol for short periods of time, if you're constantly stressed then you're constantly exposed to the hormone. And this constant exposure can lead to unwanted side effects such as weight gain. Fortunately, you can quickly and easily lower your cortisol levels by meditating.

Here now are some of the other benefits of regular meditation. Some of these benefits are a direct result of the actual act of meditating, while other benefits come from the fact that you're managing stress:

- *Lowers blood pressure and slows heart rate*. Together, these two things result in a smaller chance of having heart problems.

- *Relieves headaches*. Many headaches are tension headaches that are produced as a direct result of stress. The headache sufferer may clench her teeth, grind her teeth at night, and hold her muscles tense when she's under stress. Pretty soon that results in a headache.

People who meditate report fewer headaches, perhaps due to the relaxing effects of meditation.

- *Results in falling asleep faster and more restful sleep.* Those who meditate report falling asleep faster and enjoying more restful sleep. This is likely due to a combination of the physical benefits (such as a reduced heart rate) as well as the emotional and mental benefits (since the person isn't laying awake worrying about everything).

- *Increases serotonin levels.* Scientists have discovered that meditation increases serotonin levels. Serotonin is a hormone that affects your overall feeling of well being. People who are depressed tend to have lower serotonin levels (which is why anti-depressant medication seeks to increase this hormone). You can increase your serotonin levels naturally with meditation.

- *Alleviates premenstrual syndrome symptoms.* PMS symptoms are wide-ranging, but tend to include pain, headaches, irritability and extreme fatigue. Much of this is attributed to changing estrogen levels. However, females who meditate report fewer PMS symptoms, perhaps because meditation helps normalize hormone levels and contribute to an overall feeling of well being.

- *Helps regulate your weight.* Stress causes the release of the hormone cortisol, which is thought to make it more difficult for you to maintain a healthy weight. As mentioned previously, meditation reduces stress, which in turn reduces your cortisol levels.

But that's not all. Some people turn to overeating and "comfort food" as a means of dealing with stress. If you manage your stress through meditation, then you'll be less likely to overeat. In turn, you're less likely to gain weight.

- *Decreases pain.* Those who meditate have reported a decrease in pain, including chronic pain. This may be due in part to the body regulating and healing itself. It may also be due in part to the fact that those who meditate learn to turn their attention away from their aches and pains.

- *Slows aging.* As you know, meditation helps regulate the physical processes in the body. Once these are normalized, you become healthier, which means you aren't aging as fast. But beyond that, meditation is thought to help decrease harmful things in your body like free radicals, which can accelerate your biological aging process.

- *Increases athletic performance.* Meditation improves athletic performance for multiple reason. Perhaps the overriding reason is because those who meditate are better able to make the mind-body connection. This means you may experience improved coordination and overall better athletic ability.

However, meditation also contributes to other factors that improve performance. For example, meditation helps people sleep better. And those who can rest longer are better able to recover from strenuous workouts.

As you'll learn about in just a few moments, meditation can also help improve attention and focus, both of which are important skills for athletes to develop and sharpen.

- *Enhances the immune system and leads to faster healing.*

Meditation contributes to overall health, such as by normalizing body processes and contributing to more restful sleep. Add these benefits together, and you have a body that works better in every way – including a better immune system and faster healing.

Indeed, research even suggests that meditation helps increase the number of "killer cells" that actively attack disease in the body (including everything from common ailments like flu to more serious ailments like cancer).

We can't go so far as to say that meditation cures these diseases. But chances are, regular meditation will make you feel better... no matter what ails you.

- *Helps reduce asthma symptoms.* Asthma sufferers report fewer asthma symptoms, as meditation helps them to breathe easier. In part, this is because meditation does help reduce all sorts of tension in the body. But meditation also helps the person become more aware of how she's breathing, which can help her to start breathing more deeply.

The above list isn't an exhaustive list of the physical benefits you'll receive when you meditate. If I started to list every benefit, I could go on for pages. And that's because I could tell you how reduced stress through meditation can increase fertility

I could tell you about all the hundreds of diseases and ailments that can be improved using meditation (in part because your body and immune system will function better). These ailments include arthritis, allergies, fatigue... and so much more.

Instead, let me just sum it up for you:

Meditation is healthy. Your body will thank you.

Emotional and Psychological Benefits

Think about this for a moment: If you could create a pill that delivered all of the physical benefits described above, you'd be a millionaire! People would line up by the thousands for your little invention.

And yet you can get all of these benefits and more just by spending a few minutes each day meditating. Indeed, we haven't even covered a fraction of the benefits. Read on to discover the emotional and psychological benefits of meditation...

- *Improves your attention and focus.* The more you meditate, the more you're essentially practicing focusing your attention and focus on a singular object or concept. Due to this practice, you'll soon be able to be more attentive and focused in other parts of your life (such as at work). And as mentioned before, these sorts of benefits even spill over into your physical activities, since a focused athlete is a good athlete.

- *Increases your ability to learn and remember.* Learning and memory are directly related to your ability to focus on whatever it is you're trying to learn or remember. As such, an improvement in focus directly leads to an improvement in memory. You'll enjoy this benefit at school, at work, and in the mall parking lot the next time you need to find your car. ☺

- *Unlocks your creativity.* If you've ever brainstormed (either alone or with a group), then you already know that your best ideas aren't simmering on the surface. Usually you need to dig for them, since the worries of the day crowd your mind and won't let the good ideas through.

Indeed, if you spend 30 minutes doing a "brain dump" on paper, it's probably those last few minutes where you'll unearth the best ideas. And that's because you've finally got past the surface (the worries of the day) and into your subconscious, where your creativity is just waiting to be discovered.

Meditation helps unlock your creativity because it too seeks to get past the worries of the day. When your mind isn't constantly bubbling up with worrying thoughts and anxieties, it's easier for you to be creative.

- *Contributes to better relationships.* Have you ever noticed that when you're stressed out, it's pretty easy to take it out on those around you? You can be irritable, blaming or just generally be in a foul mood.
Because meditation helps you manage stress and manage your emotions, in turn you'll become someone that everyone enjoys being around. And that means you'll enjoy better relationships at home, at work, at school and when you're attending social events.

- *Helps put things in perspective.* You have a million little things going on in your life. Collectively, they'll all add up to stress. And so it's easy to look at one of these things individually (such as breaking a shoelace or a fingernail) as a big stressor.

  However, when you meditate you'll learn how to put these little stressors into perspective. Indeed, you'll be better able to look at the big picture – the world view – and see that you're actually quite fortunate to be living the way you do.

- *Gives you greater confidence and willpower.* Meditation isn't overly difficult.

However, it does require a commitment from you. You need to commit to doing it regularly (even if it's just for a few minutes per day). And while you're doing it, you'll need to use your powers of concentration and focus.

The more you practice, the better you'll get at meditating (and the more benefits you'll enjoy). You'll see your confidence soar, just as it would when you learn anything new and/or set and achieve a new goal. And you'll be able to take your willpower and discipline to new levels, all as a result of honing these skills through regular meditation.

- *Reduces anxiety (and phobias)*. As you've already discovered, the brain activity of someone who's meditating actually shifts away from those parts of the brain that are associated with fear and anxiety. In addition, people who are managing their stress also feel less anxious. Together, this adds up a calmer, happier you.

- *Helps you to stop worrying*. Have you ever imagined that someone you loved was "dead in the ditch" just because he was running a few minutes late? Do you have a tendency to worry about things you can't control, or blow up small worries into major dramas?

All of this is pretty common. But when you start meditating regularly, you'll find that your worries melt away. You'll stop getting anxious and worrying about the littlest things. And doing so will help contribute to your overall sense of calm, peace and wellbeing.

- *Decreases dependence on alcohol, cigarettes or other drugs.* While some people manage stress using high-calorie or otherwise unhealthy food (chocolate cake, anyone?), others turn to nicotine, alcohol and even illegal drugs in order to deal with stress.

Regular meditation can decrease dependence on all of those. Because of reduced stress levels, those who meditate are less likely to turn to drugs to manage stress. And because meditation leads to less pain and better sleep, those who meditate are also likely to become hooked on sleep aids and painkillers.

- *Reduces aggression.* Meditation helps alleviate aggression and irritability, which leads to a calmer, happier you. And in reducing aggression, you'll also be less likely to fight with your colleagues and family, engage in aggressive "road rage" behavior and similar.

Overall, meditation contributes to your sense of overall wellbeing by making you feel calmer, happier and more emotionally balanced. In turn, your decreased anxiety and decreased stress all help to contribute to your physical wellbeing (as described above).

If you want to take it a step further, you can also enjoy the spiritual benefits of meditation. Read on…

Spiritual Benefits

As mentioned before, you don't need to be a religious person to enjoy meditation. You don't even need to consider yourself to be a spiritual person. But if you are interested in spirituality, then you'll be interested in the following spiritual benefits.

NOTE: While many of these spiritual benefits may come to you just a result of calming your mind, you're likely to get the most spiritual benefit if you use "concept meditation" and similar techniques. This is where you focus on a singular concept, like god, love, forgiveness, the connectedness of all people, etc. You'll learn more about these meditation techniques just a bit later in this book.

- *Brings you closer to your god (or gods).* Some people (such as Buddhist monks) meditate for spiritual purposes. They use meditation to still their minds so that they can pray, listen for answers and come to a better

understanding of god. You can do the same thing, no matter what religion you follow.
- *Heightens awareness of yourself and others.* Meditation allows you to get past the little trivial things that don't really matter. It's then that you can start to become aware of why you act the way you do, and why others act as they do.

For example, have you ever told a lie... and even as it was coming out of your mouth, you wondered why you did it? Or have you ever hurt someone? We're not always aware of our own motives. But if you meditate, you can get an increased awareness and understanding of yourself and others.

- *Gives you the ability to open your heart for love and forgiveness.* Meditation helps you to become more open to unconditional love, forgiveness and compassion. And while you may extend love, forgiveness and compassion to others, you may find that you need to first extend it to yourself. Meditation can help you "cleanse" yourself through forgiveness and move past all the hurt and pain in your life.

- *Allows you to see the "bigger picture."* We humans are pretty selfish, in that we're always looking for the "what's in it for me" angle. When you meditate, you gain more self-awareness... and in doing so, you'll soon see that you're just a small part of the Universe.

However, you'll also see how you're connected to everyone and everything else – and that hurting someone else is really hurting yourself. You'll see the bigger picture, and how even the small things you do affect someone else.

- *Helps move you past ego issues*. Meditation will help you move past your ego issues. You may start to see that money, belongings and other material goods really aren't that important – and that all they really serve is the ego. As you move past these ego issues, you'll discover what's really important in life. Which brings us to our next benefit...

- *Helps you discover your reason for being/purpose.* Many of us have dreams of getting the fancy car and the big house with the white picket fence. In order to get these things, we go to college to get the right major so that we can land the "right" job.

  However, you may find that your desire for these sorts of material goods fades as you begin to meditate. Suddenly, the goal of acquiring as much money and material goods as possible is no longer your main goal. You'll find yourself wanting to make a difference, to contribute, and to do something meaningful with your life.

Sure, you may very well get rich following your purpose in life. But whereas many people work the job just to get the money, your actual work will be more important to you than any amount of money.

- *Opens you to new experiences.* Sometimes we set goals for ourselves, but we also want to control how we achieve those goals. When you start regularly meditating, you'll begin to see that there's more than one way to achieve any goal. And you'll also see doors open and opportunities present themselves because of your heightened sense of awareness and your open mind.

- *Brings you peace.* I've mentioned this before but it's worth repeating: meditation calms your mind and contributes to an overall sense of peace and wellbeing.

Reflect

You've just discovered the physical, emotional, psychological and spiritual benefits of meditation. You also discovered that you won't get most of these benefits overnight. It takes time. But the more regularly you meditate, the more you'll enjoy a happier, healthier you.

Now that you know how meditation can benefit you, let's take a look at the different types of meditation that you can practice…

Choosing the Best Meditation Technique

There are dozens if not hundreds of different variations of meditation for you to choose from.

In this chapter, you'll discover the two main types of meditation. Plus you'll get an overview of some of the more common variations of these two main types. Finally, you'll find out how to choose a method that's right for you.

Distinguishing Between the Two Main Types of Meditation

There are two main types of meditation you can practice:

- Concentration meditation (AKA structured meditation).
- Mindfulness meditation (AKA unstructured meditation).

Let's examine these two separately…

Concentration (Structured) Meditation

Remember earlier when I told you how experts speculate that ancient people first discovered meditation by staring into their fires? This would be a form of concentration meditation, where the person focuses on one object, one activity or even one concept.

For example, the person who's practicing concentration meditation may choose to do one of the following:

- *Focus on a sound.* Here the person may focus all of their attention on a sound such as rushing water in a river, waves lapping on a shore, water in a fountain, the wind blowing through the trees, a ringing bell or anything else. The person may shut their eyes to help block out visual information (to help them focus on the sound).

- *Focus on a (visual) object.* Here the person has their eyes open as they focus on an object. That object might be a flickering candle, a slowly swinging pendulum, a crystal or other rock, a picture or painting, a natural scene (either sitting in nature or

looking out the window), etc. If desired, the person may put on muffling headphones to help block out sounds. (Simply sitting in a quiet place works.)
- *Focus on an activity.* Here the person performs some activity – such as walking – and focuses fully on that activity. For example, the person who's meditating may focus on her arms swinging or legs moving.
However, the most common type of "activity" meditation is to focus on one's breath. Later in this book you'll discover why this is so powerful!

- *Focus on a chant.* This is where you focus on

the sound, except that you're the one making the sound. You may use a traditional chant (like "om"), or you may choose a short phrase like "I am relaxed" or "All is love." If you're spiritually minded, you chant a prayer or scripture.

- *Focus on a concept.* Finally, one of the other ways you can use concentration meditation is by focusing on a concept. Here's where you might focus on concepts such as, "What is my purpose in life?" Or you may simply focus on something like love, forgiveness, compassion, or your god.

When the mind wanders away from your singular focus, your job is refocus on your single object, sound, concept or activity. You don't do this in an abrupt way, and you don't get angry with yourself if your mind wanders. Instead, you gently refocus your mind back on whatever it is that you're focusing your concentration.

Mindfulness (Unstructured) Meditation

Mindfulness meditation is sometimes referred to as "living in the now." This is because you don't seek to focus your attention on any one single thought, object or sound. Instead, you allow your mind to wander, and you welcome all experiences.

However, here is the key: When you practice mindfulness meditation, you're a detached observer. You don't react to what you're witnessing. You don't let feelings like panic and fear well up and control you. Instead, you witness and acknowledge without judgment.

All of this sounds pretty easy, right? Here's the thing: You're used to letting your thoughts control you and create emotional reactions.

Think about it for a moment...

Have you ever suddenly remembered something during a quiet moment and you were temporarily overcome with emotion?

For example, perhaps you were taking your morning shower and suddenly you remembered that you needed to pay a late bill. Maybe you curse a little under your breath. And you probably hurry through your shower (no longer enjoying it) so you can take care of that task.

When you engage in mindfulness meditation, you become detached from the emotions. If you think of a late bill, you don't curse at yourself for not sending it in sooner – remember, there's no judgment or evaluating. You're just observing.

Instead, what you do is acknowledge the thought and move on. You don't worry about the past. You don't worry about what you need to do in the future. Instead, you live in this EXACT moment – and experience and observe everything in the current moment.

Now that you understand the difference between concentration meditation and mindfulness meditation, let's explore them further by looking at fourteen different forms of meditation…

1) Activity Meditation

Typically when you think of meditation, you think of sitting comfortably, perhaps even in a yoga-type posture. You may even close your eyes. Activity meditation, on the other hand, is just the opposite in that your eyes are open and you're performing some sort of activity.

The most common form of activity meditation is walking meditation, which I'll describe in just a moment. But do note that you can engage in all sorts of other possible activities, including:

- Yoga
- Gardening
- Bicycling
- Running
- Swimming
- Hiking
- Chores (like washing the dishes)

And so on. Repetitive activities work best.

Whatever activity you choose, the point is to focus on the activity itself. Pay attention to the way your body feels. Pay attention to the work in front of you. Pay attention to what you feel (but do not become attached to any feelings).

TIP: Depending on what activity you choose and your approach to this activity, you can turn this into either a concentration or a mindfulness exercise. It really depends on whether you focus your attention to one aspect of the activity, or whether you are "in the now" and observing the entire experience. In most cases, you'll probably be engaging in a form of mindfulness meditation.

Let me show you how this works by using walking meditation as an example, since walking meditation is one of the more popular forms of activity meditation...

You may begin your meditation even before you take your first step. When you stand up, pay attention to the sensations in the bottom of your feet. Become aware of how your body feels. Pay attention to how your muscles work automatically to keep your balance.

Wait, is that your cell phone ringing? Oh for goodness' sake, shut it off. Leave it at home. You don't want any distractions. Your job is to focus on walking... (And no, you can't invent a "cell phone meditation" or "texting meditation.") ☺

OK. Are you ready? Let's continue...

Start walking. Don't walk at an abnormal pace, as you want this to feel comfortable. Now pay attention to the sensations in your body. Start with the bottom of your foot. Pay attention to the way your toes, heels and soles feel as they hit the ground. Listen to the sound they make.

Move up to your ankles. Pay attention to how they feel with each step. Feel their strength as they help keep you upright and in balance.

Continue on moving up your body, paying attention to the sensations at every part of your body. Feel the wind on your skin. Pay attention to how your clothes come in contact with your body. Relax your eyes as you walk so that everything is slightly out of focus.

Pay attention to your breathing. Don't try to control it. Instead, just become aware of it. Pay attention to how many breaths you take per footstep. If it feels comfortable, create a pattern of two or three footsteps per breath, so that you have a regular beat. Don't alter your breathing – instead, alter your footsteps.

While this is primarily a concentration form of meditation, some people use it as a mindfulness meditation. That means they are still very much aware of their body, their breathing and the activity. But they also take in the whole experience, but becoming aware of their surroundings and becoming aware of their emotions, thoughts and other inner states.

> *TIP: However, here's the key: If you're using mindfulness meditation, you're observing without judgment or attachment. You observe the world as*

if you were watching clouds go by.

Walking meditation can be done almost anywhere at any time. You can get in a few minutes of walking meditation if you park your car just a bit further away at work, college or even at the mall.

2) Concept Meditation

Concept meditation is a type of concentration meditation. Instead of focusing on an object or even an activity, you focus on a concept.

Set aside at least 15 minutes of quiet time for yourself. If you have other people living in your house, make sure they know you need to remain undisturbed. Get into some comfortable clothes and set the mood in whatever way pleases you.

Then get into a position that's comfortable for you – you may sit, recline or even lay down. Relax. Breathe. And then start thinking about a concept. Other thoughts may pass into your mind, but you need to just acknowledge them and let them go (like letting a balloon go so that it floats away).

What concept should you think about? It's up to you. But obviously, you shouldn't think about something upsetting like, "Am I going to get kicked out on the street if I can't make the mortgage this month?" And of course thinking meditating on whether Tiger Woods is still the best golfer probably isn't a constructive use of your time.

Instead, you may think about vague concepts. You may meditate on simple things as a way to gain a new perspective and a new understanding.

Below are just a few examples of concepts you can focus on for your concept meditation. You may use one of these ideas, or meditate on your own concepts:

- Love.
- The greater meaning of the changing of the seasons.
- How you are connected with everyone and everything.
- Forgiveness.
- Compassion.
- Altruism.
- Birth.
- Death.
- A passage from your holy book (Koran, Bible, etc).
- God (Buddha, Allah, etc).
- Silence.
- What it is to "be."
- Unconditional acceptance.
- Healing.

- Nature (such as the rainbow following the rain, or a butterfly emerging from a cocoon).
- Universal consciousness.
- Those who came before you.
- Trust.
- Letting go.
- Kindness.
- Good.
- Evil.
- Fire.
- Heaven or Hell.
- Emptiness.
- Silence.
- The life force.
- Mother.
- Father.
- Light and energy.
- Peace.

And so on. We'll elaborate on some of these concept meditations (such as death) just a little later in this list of meditation techniques.

3) Yoni Mudra Meditation

You are getting a constant barrage of information from your five senses. Even if you're still and quiet, your brain is taking in an enormous amount of information and processing it. Yoni Mudra seeks to shut down your senses to stop some of the flow of information from the outside world so that you can focus on what's going on in your "inside world."

Stop reading this book for a moment and just pay attention to everything that's going on around you.

- What do hear? The computer humming, people and pets walking around, traffic, the wind, the ticking of a clock.

- What do you see? Even though you're focusing on the monitor right in front of you, you're taking in far more visual information. You're seeing colors and movements not just right in front of you, but well to your sides (peripheral vision). And your mind needs to process all this information.

- What do you smell? Your clothing, furniture, your house. The wet dog. The trash that needs to go out. The fresh paint. Dust. Soap.

- What do you taste? Toothpaste. Your lunch. Coffee. Soda.

- What do you feel? You can feel the clothing on

your skin, the sensations of the chair against your body, an itchy bug bite, your hair tickling your cheek and so on.

See what I mean? Even if you more or less ignore much of what's going on around you, your body is still sending the information to your brain, and your brain is still hard at work processing it all.

That's where Yoni Mudra meditation comes in. Here you use your hands to close off several of your senses.

Lift both your hands in front of your face, palms facing you, fingers facing each other, thumbs pointing up. Now put your hands to your face. Plugs your ears with your thumbs. Close your eyes with your index fingers. Plug your nostrils with your middle fingers.

Use your last two fingers to pull your lips together.

As you inhale and exhale, move your fingers to allow your breath to flow through your lips or nostrils freely.

Once you've slowed the information, then you can use some form of concentration meditation (such as breath meditation or concept meditation).

4) Basic Breath Meditation

Breath meditation is another of the more common meditations. And it's also very powerful, because your breath is a powerful part of meditating. Indeed, later in this book we'll talk about the power of breath, no matter what type of meditation form you're practicing.

For now, however, let's talk about a simple breath meditation. This is a form of concentration meditation, where you put all your attention and focus on your breath.
Start by setting aside some quiet time for yourself, slipping into some comfortable clothing and finding a place to relax where you won't be interrupted.

Some practitioners suggest that you help clear your mind by starting with a chant, such as, "Everyone deserves love and true happiness." Do this for a minute or two.

> *TIP: This isn't a mantra or concept meditation, so you don't keep chanting. Instead, you're helping to cultivate the right attitude and mindset before you officially begin your breath meditation. It's during these first few minutes that the other "thoughts*

du jour" may barrel into your mind like a freight train, so you can use these few minutes to help acknowledge and then clear you mind of these distracting thoughts.

Now you begin with the actual breath meditation. Breathe in and out deliberately, perhaps slower and deeper than normal. But don't force it or breathe in a way that's uncomfortable.

TIP: Imagine you're breathing the purest air in the world. Now how would you breathe this clean, pure air if you knew you could only breathe it for 15 more minutes before you'd be thrown into a stuffy, dirty dungeon? You'd savor each breath, right? That's how you should be breathing during your breath meditation... as if every breath was your last breath of pure, clean air.

Pay attention to your breath as you inhale and exhale. Choose one point to focus on, such as the way it feels as your lungs fill up and then deflate. Or you may choose to focus on the point of entry and exit, as you feel your breath moving across your lips or nostrils. Choose the point that's most comfortable for you.

If your mind wanders from your breathing (and it will), gently refocus your mind. Think of yourself as a gentle collie dog who's patiently herding sheep. There's always one sheep that keeps wandering away – much the way you always have thoughts wandering away from your chosen focus – but you just keep gently leading your focus and thoughts back to your breath.

5) Death Meditation

This is a form of concentration meditation. More specifically, it's a form of concept meditation. And some may consider this a form of creepy meditation, but that's neither here nor there. ☺

You've heard the saying that only two things are inevitable in life: Death and taxes. I've certainly never heard of anyone doing a tax meditation (as meditation is pointless if you fall asleep!), but there are avid fans of the death meditation.

Because death is inevitable, and because it's a natural process, some people choose to experience it while they're conscious. It's meeting death before you actually die. It's a way to connect to your true self (to your soul), to the root of your existence.

Here's why: After you die, you have nothing. You can't take your body with you. You can't take your iPhone or your Wii or your car. You can't take your loved ones or your college degree or this book. All you have is your true essence. So when you do a death meditation, you're essentially connecting yourself with your true essence.

Just as with other meditations, you need to set aside time where you can be alone and uninterrupted. Get into comfortable clothing and sit or lay down in a way that's comfortable. (Laying down is preferable for the death meditation, as it's more corpselike than sitting.)

In order to calm your mind, you may want to start with a basic meditation such as breath meditation. Let the cares of the day float away so that you can focus on first your breath… and then the concept of death. Or if you prefer, use a body scan meditation (described a bit later in this book) to help you through the initial relaxation.

Once you are completely relaxed, then you may begin the actual death meditation. As you might suspect, it begins with you imagining yourself dying.

Now, you don't just carelessly think about the concept of dying. You don't just let the image of a dead you pop briefly into your mind. Instead, you fully immerse yourself in the experience and imagine every stage of the dying process. And you imagine it in great detail...

Imagine the energy (the life force) slowly leaving every part of your body. The heart slows. The blood no longer surges through your body. Every cell, every tiny part of your body, is slowly shutting down. And in turn, your organs are slowing and then stopping. You lose the ability to move as the muscles slow and die. Your breath slows and eventually ceases.

In short, imagine what it will feel like in every part of your body as you die.

Now you turn your attention to your consciousness. Your body – the physical you – has died for all practical purposes. That means that your thoughts and emotions no longer have any relevance. Ponder on that fact. Meditate on the idea that your hopes, dreams, desires and other thoughts do not matter any more.

You are no more. The physical you no longer exists (think ashes to ashes). All that's left is the spiritual you, your essence. And it's this essence that you should spend the next 15 or 20 minutes meditating on. This is the true you, the part that goes on even after death.

When you've completed this meditation of your essence, don't just jump up like your pants are on fire. Instead, you need to come out of it slowly.

One way to do this is to simply imagine in great detail the opposite process. That is, imagine the life force re-entering your body. You can imagine every organ, muscle, tissue, vein and cell coming back to life. Your breath starts up again. Your thoughts and your emotions return to make you whole.

Then, slowly, you may focus on the "here and now" and end your meditation.

6) Energy Meditation

Energy is another form of concept meditation, where you

put your sole focus on the idea of the energy around you.
(Although you can easily turn this into a mindfulness exercise, if you focus less on the concept and more on the actual feeling of the energy.)

As usual, find a quiet comfortable place and set aside 15 to 30 minutes. Get into a relaxed position. Turn off all cell phones, TV, iPod and other distractions. Spend a few minutes getting relaxed, perhaps by starting with a basic breath meditation.

Now turn your attention to the concept of energy. Think about how everything is made up of energy. Think of the energy required to inhale and expel the breath from your body. Focus on the energy in the room. Feel it surrounding you, hugging you. Then expand your imagination to think of the energy in your region, your country, the earth...

and eventually the entire universe.

Think of how you are a part of this energy field. Merge into it, like a bucket of water being poured into the ocean. Feel the energy of others. Allow your energy to reach out to them. Grow bigger because you are a part of everything.

7) Dualistic Meditation

Here's another type of concept meditation. The idea is to focus on your dual nature without judgment, and then accept it.

Everything has a dual nature. We think of the most obvious opposites, like male and female, black and white, hot and cold. But we can think of the dual nature of our personality or even of other objects. For example, the heat of your oven can burn you or it can cook your dinner.

Often, we tend to attach value judgments to one of the categories. And in doing so, we are actually labeling something as "bad." For example, the oven that cooks is good. The oven that burns is bad.

We turn these same judgments to ourselves. We slice up the parts of ourselves and label them. We say greed is bad. Generosity is good. Pride is good when we're proud of others. Pride is shameful when we're proud of ourselves.

What happens when you label a part of yourself as bad? You try to change that part of yourself. But in the case of duality, you can't change it. It is what it is. And so some people try to deny that part of themselves. And if that doesn't work, they feel shameful about their dual nature.

A dualistic meditation allows you to examine your dual nature, realize that it's natural, and then accept it. For example, the oven exists with the potential to burn or cook. And you exist with a multitude of personality characteristics that exist next to each other (such as selfishness and altruism).

For this meditation, you can relax as always using a basic breath meditation or similar. Then take a dual concept – such as greed/selfishness and generosity – and imagine them as a circle. Where one ends the other begins. They are not on the opposite sides of a line with distinct stopping points. They merge together in this circle... and inside of you. They are neither good nor bad. They just are.

8) Transcendental Meditation™

When you first heard about meditation, you probably heard the term Transcendental Meditation™. And that's because this is perhaps one of the most widely recognized and widely taught forms of meditation.

Transcendental Meditation™ is generally practiced twice per day for about 20 minutes for each session. However, Transcendental Meditation™ (also known by the abbreviation TM) is different because it doesn't fall into either of the two main categories of mindfulness or concentration meditation. It's often described as "restful awareness," and is generally reported to be fairly effortless.

TIP: Indeed, TM proponents say you're doing the opposite of a concentration meditation.

Concentration requires effort to focus. TM practitioners say you should just quiet the mind and let it be – only then can you dive into its depths.

The second thing that makes TM different from other types of meditation is that its experts say you cannot learn it from a book. Instead, you can only learn TM from a certified teacher who's willing to take you through a multi-day seven-step procedure. This procedure involves a personal interview, lecture instructions and then learning the actual technique. It culminates in a special ceremony.

Transcendental Meditation™ starts with a mantra, which is selected by your certified TM instructor. Generally, this mantra has no recognizable meaning to you, which allows your mind to quiet itself. As you meditate, your thoughts will "transcend" and you'll bring thoughts from the subconscious mind to the conscious mind.

> *TIP: I told you in the beginning of this book that I wouldn't send you off to find a guru (unless you wanted to do that). Here's one of those instances. If you want to learn more about TM and experience it for yourself, you'll need to find a certified instructor. Fortunately, you probably won't have to go too far to find one, especially if you live in a bigger city. You may start your search at the official TM site, www.TM.org.*

9) Mantra Meditation

Mantra meditation is fairly popular, which is why many people automatically assume that anyone who meditates must be practicing mantra meditation (which is also sometimes called vibrational meditation).

The first step is to choose a word or a sound, which will become the focus of this particular form of concentration meditation. You can choose a word that has meaning to you, like peace, serenity or love. You may choose a short phrase, like "I am love" or "I am free." Or you may choose a sound (like the infamous "om"). Whatever you choose, be sure it's a word or sound that you like, and one that you're comfortable repeating.

> *TIP: Try out a few different words before you do a mantra meditation for the first time. Say the words and see how they feel. Pay attention to the way words roll off your tongue. Check to see if you get an emotional*

response. Then for your meditation you can choose the word that gave you the best feeling.

Typically, you say your mantra out loud repeatedly. You don't need to do this loudly. Say it at a level that's comfortable for you, perhaps a whisper. You may focus on the sound. You may focus on the way your breath and lips come together to form the word or the sound.

TIP: If you begin to instead focus not on the sound but rather on the meaning of the word or the sound, then you're doing a concept meditation. In that case, you can say your word out loud say it inside your head.

10) Body Scan Meditation

Body scan meditation can be used by itself as a way for you to better connect your body and mind. Indeed, regularly practicing this form of meditation helps you recognize stress and tension as it first starts building up in your body (so that you can better manage and alleviate it before it becomes a problem). You can also use this type of meditation as a "warm up" to other types of meditation (such as the previously described death meditation).

As usual, find a quiet place and set aside uninterrupted time. Be sure to close yourself off from any distractions such as phones, alarms, visitors, TV, etc. Also, get into some comfortable, loose-fitting clothing.

While you can practice the body scan meditation in a relaxed sitting or reclining position if you so choose, ideally you should lay down on your back. Close your eyes, focus on your breath for a few minutes and relax.

When you're ready to begin, start at your toes and focus fully on the sensations you feel in your toes. You may even increase the tension in your toes and then immediately relax them, just so you can experience the difference between tension and relaxation.

Now continue on, doing the same with other parts of your feet. Pay attention to the sensations in the soles of your feet, the top of your feet and your ankles. Feel the pressure point where your feet come in contact with the surface of the floor, the mat, your bed, the couch, the ground or whatever it is your laying on. Tense your muscles slightly in your feet… and then pay attention to how relaxed those parts are.

Now move up to the calves of your legs. Feel them come into contact with the surface you're laying on. Tense the muscles. Then let them relax and focus on how they feel when they're relaxed.

Move to your knees. Then up to your pelvis and hips. Feel the tension in those parts of your body. Become aware of it. Then consciously seek to release it.

Now you're at your abdomen and on up to your chest. Tense and release, paying attention to first the tension... and then the resultant relaxation. Feel the clothing touching your skin. Focus on how your breath expands and contracts your chest.

Focus on the muscles and tension in your back. Tense and release, paying attention to the sensations in your body and the pressure points. Then move to your shoulders… your elbows… your wrist… your fingers.

Finally, to your neck and then your head. Purse your lips and jaw and then release, paying attention to how it feels as the tension melts away. Relax your eyes.

At this point you should be completely relaxed as well as very in tune with your body. You may continue to just focus on your body sensations, such as the pressure points, the deep relaxation, the warmth (or cold) of the room as it flows over you.

Alternatively, you can now begin a different type of meditation. You may practice breath meditation, concept meditation (such as death or energy meditation), or anything else that suits you.

11) Eating Meditation

As you've already discovered, you can choose to do almost anything when you decide to do an activity meditation – eating is no exception. And depending on how you approach your eating meditation, it may become either a concentration meditation (if, for example, you focus on the concept of eating) or it may become a mindfulness exercise (if you instead allow yourself to experience the activity).

For example, let's suppose you decide to eat an orange. You can engage in a mindfulness meditation if you pay attention to every step of this activity. Pay attention to the sensation of the peel underneath your fingernails. Listen to the sound it makes as you pull back the peel. Focus on the "burst" of pleasant orange aroma.

Then put a piece of the orange in your mouth. Roll it over your tongue. Squeeze it gently between your teeth and let the juices drip out slowly. Pay attention to the taste as well as the sensations of the orange inside your mouth.

Alternatively, you may use this as a concept meditation where you sit quietly and focus on the orange, thinking about how it came to be in front of you. You may imagine it from a small seed to growing on a tree to being plucked when it's ripe and ready.

12) Writing Meditation

Most meditation practices have you quiet the mind. You don't want your mind to go blank, but rather you want to focus on a particular object or concept (as is the case with concentration meditation), or you want to put your energies into focusing on the experience of being in the now (mindfulness meditation). You can do either of these when you practice writing meditation.

When you practice writing meditation, you're allowing your subconscious thoughts to become conscious. Once again, you are moving past the worries of the day. You don't concern yourself with the past or the future. Rather you focus on being in the now.

In other words – a writing meditation is very similar to other types of meditations, except that you are basically making a record of your session. Here are two examples:

- *Concept-oriented writing meditation.* Here you can focus on a concept (see concept meditation for a nice list of concepts for you to choose from). Instead of sitting quietly and thinking about the concept, you write whatever it is you're thinking about.

- *Mindfulness-oriented writing meditation.* Here you meditate and just focus on living in the now – except that you write rather than just experiencing it silently. However, the same rules apply here as in regular mindfulness meditation. That means you can't attach judgments to whatever it is you're thinking about. Rather, you need to be a detached observer.

> *TIP: The whole "detached observer" thing throws a lot of*

people. As mentioned before, you need to treat your thoughts like clouds that you're simply watching pass by. Or think of yourself as watching a movie, where you're watching someone else's thoughts and feelings pass by. You acknowledge and are aware of them, but you don't become attached to them, nor do you judge them.

ANOTHER TIP: Some people find it easier to focus when they do a writing meditation as opposed to doing a simple meditation. Perhaps that's because we live in a society where we need to always be on the move and doing something. Because we're so used to constant motion, our minds wander too easily when we just sit quietly.

Granted, the whole point of practicing any form of meditation is so that you CAN learn to set aside all the worries and stressors and just live in the moment (or focus on something else). The idea is to quiet the mind. However, you may find it easier to quiet your mind by starting with a writing meditation and then moving to other forms of meditation later.

Whatever you choose and whatever happens, just be sure not to get frustrated or beat up on yourself if you can't keep focused. Just keep taking small steps towards your goals. A few minutes of quiet meditation per day (even if your mind does wander) is better than no meditation. And besides, you'll do a little better tomorrow when you sit down and try it again.

13) Chakra Meditation

First, a side note: If you're mainly interested in basic meditations like the very relaxing breath and body scan meditations, then some of these other forms of meditation may give you pause. Chakra meditation in particular may get you cocking your eyebrow a bit skeptically, especially if you're not familiar with chakra and energy work.

And that's ok. If this isn't your cup of tea, you can skip it. My goal here to give you a wide overview of the different types of meditations. That way, you can explore further those that interest you. Or you can just stick with the basic meditations as described in this book.

Now back to chakra meditation…

In order to understand this type of meditation, you need to know a bit about chakras (which means "wheel"). When we talk about chakras, we're referring to the seven rotating (wheel like) energy points on the body, including the:

- Crown chakra (top of the head)
- Third Eye / Brow chakra (between and just above your eyes)
- Throat chakra
- Heart chakra
- Solar plexus chakra (navel)
- Sacral chakra (prostrate / ovaries)
- Base chakra (coccyx)

All of these chakras are thought to be associated with different colors and different functions of the body, mind and spirit.

Although chakras are talked about in many places throughout history, they're most known for being referred to in the context of medicine – especially Chinese medicine and Western alternative medicine (e.g., energy work).

That's because it's thought that if your chakras are open and in balance, you'll feel good and be healthy. But if they are not in balance – or if there seems to be some sort of "clog" that's hindering the free flow of the energy – then you'll feel sick, listless, anxious, irritable and so on.

Now, there are more than a dozen common chakra meditations (and no doubt countless variations). But the general idea is to focus on your life force (energy) either by meditating on the energy coming from each of your chakras or by focusing on just one chakra.

TIP: If you'd rather use a guided meditation, check out the meditations on http://www.YourBestMeditation.com I personally use and recommend. Otherwise, below you'll find an overview of a general chakra meditation…

If you want to focus on all seven chakras, then start at the lower chakra (the coccyx/sacral chakra) and just imagine pure energy flowing freely in and out of that chakra. Spend a few minutes doing the same thing for each chakra as you work your way up your body. Then work your way back down, focusing for perhaps 30 to 60 seconds once again on the energy flowing in and out of this chakra. Be mindful of the experience and how your actual physical body feels as you focus on each point of your body.

Alternatively, you may wish to just focus on one chakra. For example, you may put all your focus on your brow (third eye) chakra, which is associated with intuition. You may begin your meditation with a simple breath or body scan meditation to relax. Then put all your attention on your brow chakra. Feel it opening up. Allow yourself to imagine the energy flowing in and out. Imagine as your intuition and awareness heighten in response.

14) Zen Meditation

If Transcendental Meditation isn't the first type of meditation that springs to mind, chances are you thought of Zen meditation. And that's because this too is one of the more widely known and widely practiced forms of meditation, perhaps because it was popularized by Buddhist monks.

TIP: When you hear about Zen meditation, you'll often hear reference to zazen. This is a Japanese word that refers to seated meditation.

Zen meditation is a type of mindfulness meditation, as the point is to live fully in the moment. When you sit down to meditate (especially those advanced practitioners), you are in fact sitting just for the sake of sitting. You're letting go of everything else – the past and the future – so that you can live totally in the now.

SIDE BAR: Here again, you can see why it's sometimes hard for beginners to start meditating. Rarely (if ever) do we just sit for the sake of sitting in our fast-paced society! We're always reliving our past hurts or past glories. Or we're thinking about what fun we're going to have next or worrying about things in the future.

As an example, think of a small child ripping open presents at birthday party. As he's opening one present, he's looking over at the rest of them, wondering what they might be! He's not even enjoying the process of opening presents, because he's always thinking of the next present... rather than enjoying the one that's in his hands.

It's not just small children that do this – we all do! When you have a few moments of quiet time, what do you think about?

When you have a conversation with friends, what do you talk about? I'll eat my hat if you tell me that your thoughts and conversations are always focused solely on the present moment! ☺

Learning to live in the moment is (for some people) the whole point of practicing meditation, especially Zen meditation! We can't do anything about the past. The future isn't here yet. All we have is this moment, right now... so why not fully experience it?

Zazen starts with you getting into a sitting position. Some people will use the common yoga or meditation postures such as the cross-legged half lotus. However, you don't have to use this posture if it's not comfortable. Instead, you can simply sit in comfortable chair if you'd like.

Side note: The half lotus position (and similar positions) were likely popularized by those people who sit cross-legged often. As such, they were comfortable in this position, so it made sense for them to meditate in that position as well!

Point is, you don't have to bend yourself like a pretzel to reap all the benefits of meditation.

Now the point of Zen meditation is to realize that body, breath and body are one and the same. To gain awareness of this, relax your body and start focusing on your breaths. To ensure that your mind doesn't wander, slowly count from one to ten as you inhale and exhale.

There are several variations you can use here. You can take a deep inhale and count out a long one (ooooonnnnneeeee), and then exhale slowly and count out a long two (ttttwwwwoooo). Alternatively, you can count one on the inhale, exhale slowly and then count two on the next inhale (and so on). Or you can reverse that by counting one on the exhale, breathing in deeply, and then counting two on the next exhale.

It doesn't really matter which one you choose. What does matter is that you keep counting with your breaths (and that you breathe slowly and deeply). If your mind wanders (and it will!), then go back to one and start counting up to ten again.

This isn't a competition. That means you shouldn't pull out a scorecard and mark down the numbers of counting sets you do before your mind wanders. Instead, the counting is there to keep your mind focused on both the numbers and your breathing.

It's easy to recognize when your mind wanders when you're doing something like counting, because suddenly you won't be so sure of the last number you counted (and/or you realize you're just counting absentmindedly on autopilot). When you catch yourself doing that (e.g., your mind is wandering), acknowledge the thought and release it. Then go back to one and start all over.

TIP: Once you have mastered zazen, then most people move on to the next step, which is where you truly sit for the sake of sitting. However, don't look at this as some competition to move on to the advance phases. The breath-counting exercises are just as important and beneficial as the advanced meditation exercises.

Reflect, Plus Which Type of Meditation is Right for You?

You've just discovered the two main types of meditation (mindfulness and concentration) along with more than a dozen forms of meditation that fall into these two categories. So which type of meditation should you pursue?

There is no right or wrong answer here. And indeed, you may want to sample from this smorgasbord of meditation techniques to find out which ones you like the best.

Best of all, you aren't limited to just one. Nor are you limited by the general guidelines presented here as we talked about these different types of meditation. You can use different types of meditation on different days – or even different types on the same day!

For example, you may start your day with a simple breath meditation. In the evening, you may practice an activity meditation, such as walking. Tomorrow you may do a concept meditation.

Point is, this isn't a one-size-fits-all activity. You'll get the physical, emotional, psychological and spiritual benefits no matter what type of meditation you choose. You can start with a basic meditation (which we'll talk about in the next chapter)... and feel free to include any variations.

Next, you'll discover how to get started doing basic meditation...

Getting Started: The Basics of Simple Meditation

You've received a good overview of meditation and some of its various forms.

Now it's time to dive into the topic headfirst.

We'll start with a look at how to approach meditation, then we'll move on to the preparations you need to make before you start meditating, and finally you'll learn how to sit, breathe and focus during your meditation sessions.

Approaching Meditation: Attitude and Mindset

I've made it pretty clear throughout this book that this is a somewhat lighthearted guide to meditation for everyday folks. And even though I'm not asking you to sit around in long, flowing robes and say "om" (unless you want to), I do have to ask you to adopt a certain attitude and mindset.

You see, one reason we dispelled the myths at the beginning of this book was to help wipe out any negative connotations you might be attaching to the word "meditation." Almost every "average" person I meet seems to believe some of the myths about meditation. And it's simply not a good idea to carry that negative baggage to your meditation session.

That's because meditation won't work if your heart isn't in it.

Sure, the simple act of setting aside a few minutes each day and sitting quietly is bound to have some good effects. Any sort of quiet "me time" certainly helps with stress management and all the problems associated with stress. But if you use this "me time" for actual meditation, you'll reap far greater benefits.

Think of it this way…

Imagine you're thirsty. You're throat is parched, your lips dry. You look out the window and notice it's raining. So here's your grand idea: You'll quench your thirst by going outside, opening your mouth and tilting your head back so you can catch the raindrops.

Will that quench your thirst? Maybe. But it sure takes extra effort, extra time, and it makes you all wet to boot. It would be a whole lot easier to just turn on your kitchen tap and quickly enjoy as many glasses of water as you please.

Likewise, simply sitting quietly each day as a path to better health is like catching rain drops to quench your thirst: It helps, but it takes a long time! Instead, you can accelerate the process (and drink up the benefits by the glassful!) by using your time to practice meditation.

Since reaping the benefits begins with you approaching meditation with the right attitude and mindset, let's look at some meditation dos and don'ts to help you cultivate the right mindset:

- ***Don't view meditation as a chore***. Meditation is something you do for yourself. It's something that will make you feel relaxed, yet rejuvenated. And you'll enjoy all the physical, emotional and spiritual benefits when you practice it regularly.

Still, it's common for people who are just getting started with meditation to view it as a chore (especially your first few sessions). That's because you need to set aside time to do it, and that block of time might be a time you'd normally do something else to relax (such as watch TV). And if you've never experienced the benefits of meditation, setting aside time to do it feels a bit like you're missing out on something else.

This feeling will pass. Once you start meditating regularly, you'll get to a point where you'll feel like you're depriving yourself if you don't meditate! So set aside time and just do it. And if those first few sessions feel like a chore, go back to the beginning of this book to rediscover all the benefits you'll get when you meditate regularly.

- ***Don't feel like you're being forced to meditate***. Are you the one who's interested in meditating? Or do you have a spouse or friend who decided to meditate and is "forcing" you to meditate too?

  Meditation works best when you voluntarily commit to meditating. If you feel forced, read the benefits at the beginning of this book to help motivate you. If that doesn't make you any more willing to do it, then talk to the person who's trying to force you.

- ***Don't turn meditation into a competition***.

Sometimes when we start meditating we turn it into a competition. If we're meditating with others, we compete with them. But even if you're meditating alone, it's pretty easy to turn it into a competition.

For example, we compete with ourselves (or others) to see how long we can sit still, what sort of interesting experiences we have, how low our blood pressure drops the next time we go to the doctor's office, how many minutes or hours each day we spend in meditation... and more.

A friend tells you that he's going to start meditating too, and suddenly you hear yourself saying, "I bet I meditate twice as long as you do this week."

You're doing a breath-counting meditation, and suddenly you break your focus because you realize this is the longest you've ever sat in complete focus. (Well, up until the point your mind started marveling at your amazing feat! ☺)

Obviously, viewing meditation as a competition can break your focus even as you sit and meditate. But even if your competition exists outside of your meditation sessions, they're harmful. You'll start meditating not because you want to, but because you want to beat a record. And if you develop this competitive mindset, it will almost always seep into your sessions... meaning your mind is always somewhere else.

- ***Don't develop a superior attitude***. You may find that meditation comes really easy to you. And you may notice the benefits immediately. Suddenly, you want everyone around you to meditate too.

  That's not a bad thing. However, if you start judging people who don't view meditation the same way as you do, then you're crossing a line. If you develop a super attitude – if you think you're special because you meditate – then you're not approaching meditation with the right attitude.

- ***Don't rush through your meditation sessions***. You may be learning meditation to help you manage stress. And if you're stressed out, then your time is likely limited since you always have so much going on in your life.

Nonetheless, you need to set aside a "non rushed" time to meditate. This may mean getting up earlier in the morning before the rush of the day begins. It may mean heading to your bedroom an extra 30 minutes earlier in the evening so you can wind down from the day and meditate.

Whatever you do, don't squeeze your initial sessions between important or stressful events. For example, don't attempt to meditate for the first time ever right before you give a big presentation at work. And don't squeeze in a few minutes of meditation when you're already running late for work.

If you try to meditate during a worrying, stressful or otherwise hectic time, your mind will wander. Indeed, when you first start meditating your mind will wander no matter when you do. But why make it difficult by scheduling meditation at a time when your mind is sure to wander?

Instead, you may find it easier to schedule your meditation sessions at times when you are already somewhat relaxed (such as in the evening when you're home from work and the household chores are done). Doing so means you'll likely focus on your meditation rather than thinking about what you need to do.

TIP: Later on when you've been meditating regularly (and thus you have more control on your thoughts and your ability to relax), you may actually find it comforting and helpful to meditate right before a stressful activity. In that case, you may feel rushed before you begin – but once you begin, you'll quickly calm your mind.

However, I don't recommend this for beginners. If you start off by meditating during stressful times, you'll just get frustrated because your mind wanders almost ceaselessly. You may feel like it "doesn't work." And you may be tempted to give up on meditation entirely.

Think of it this way...

Do you remember learning how to ride a bike? You probably had training wheels for a while. If not, then you probably started out with your mom or dad running along beside you. Either way, I'm also guessing that you learned how to ride on a smooth, flat surface.

Point is, your first experience on a bike did not include going down a muddy, slippery, rock-strewn mountain trail. Doing so would have discouraged you, injured you, and maybe even scared you away from riding a bike ever again.

So just as you learn to ride a bike on a smooth, flat surface, your first meditation sessions should be completed during low-stress times.

- ***Don't start your session with any expectations.*** This tends to be a particular problem for those who are doing meditation in the hopes of achieving spiritual benefits. They approach meditation with high expectations, hoping to have one of those amazing experiences where they become enlightened, their god speaks to them, etc. You can probably see the problem already. If you come with expectations, then your mind will wander to those expectations as you're meditating.

- ***Don't analyze every step of the process.*** Here's another common problem. Instead of living in the moment while meditating, the mind wanders as the person who's meditating analyzes the process. Suddenly he or she is thinking things like, "Am I doing this right? Should I be feeling this way? Am I breathing too fast? Is this the right posture?"

Point is, analyzing the process as it happens means you're thinking about something else (and not focusing on your meditation). If you feel these thoughts rise up while you're meditating, acknowledge them and then let them go. You can revisit those thoughts later when you're no longer meditating. But don't analyze the process as you perform it.

- ***Do cultivate patience.*** If you've paid any attention to this book at all, then you already know that regular meditation provides you with all sort of physical, emotional, psychological and spiritual benefits. However, as you've also learned, these benefits don't all come to you immediately. You'll likely enjoy some benefits the very first time you meditate, but others develop over time.

That means you need to be patient. Don't expect your heart attack risk to drop overnight. Don't expect to get instant illumination in spiritual matters. Don't expect your irritability to just melt away like snow in July.

These things will come, but it takes time.

Think of it like building a house. If you get an idea for a house today and start building it tomorrow, it won't be done by the day after. Instead, you need to patiently draw up the blueprints and lay down a good foundation. Only then can you start building.

While your skeletal building structure provides some benefits (such as shelter from the rain), it will take weeks to become fully weatherproof. And it will take weeks after that before you have all the comforts of home such as windows, doors, electricity, flooring and so on.

Point is, you can't skip from learning about meditation today to reaping all the benefits tomorrow. Those things will come in time. But you need to develop patience and build your foundation.

- ***Do open your mind***. While some people approach meditation with great expectations that hinder their success, others have the opposite problem. Namely, they approach meditation with skepticism and fear.

But here's the thing: Meditation won't work if you're skeptical. Just as the person who doesn't want to be hypnotized can't be hypnotized, the person who's skeptical or fearful about meditation (perhaps to the point where he thinks it won't work) won't be able to meditate.

It's easy to see why. Meditation requires effort to calm your body, calm your mind, and point your mind in particular direction. If instead you're spending your time thinking, "Yeah right, this won't work," you're only getting distracted. And it indeed, it becomes a self-fulfilling prophecy in that the person who thinks it won't work proves himself right! (But only because he won't put in the focus to make it work.)

Likewise, fear can wreak havoc on your meditation sessions. If you're still holding on to fearful myths, you need to reread the myth section of this book to alleviate those fears.

Furthermore, don't attempt any meditation techniques that you're not comfortable with. For example, if you think the death meditation is frightening, then don't do it! Instead, do a simple breath meditation. Or if you want to do a concept meditation, then focus on something you find pleasant, like love.

Overall, you need to approach meditation with a healthy attitude and open mind.

If you're thinking meditation is "dumb," then you'll be too distracted to get into the experience. If you're so stressed you're pulling out your hair, that is not the best moment to sit down for your first-ever meditation session. And if you expect all of your problems to dissolve immediately, you'll walk away disappointed.

Be patient. Approach it with an open mind. Prepare to spend time improving with practice (rather than mastering it immediately). Do this, and you'll find meditation to be extremely relaxing and rewarding.

Now let's turn our attention to motivation and meditation...

Motivating Yourself to Meditate

There are a lot of things that we should do for a healthy mind and body, yet we neglect them. Sometimes we neglect doing these things even when we enjoy them or otherwise derive benefit! For example, how many times have you chosen to eat something unhealthy, even though you knew it would make you feel sluggish later on? And how many times have you skipped exercising, even though you knew you would feel great once you started?

The same goes for meditation. You may find there are times when you think you'll skip your meditation session "just this once." But skipping it one day can lead to skipping it another day. Then you skip it several days, which turns into a week. And all the while you rationalize that you'll get back to it "tomorrow."

This sort of behavior is fairly common with any activity you'd like to turn into a habit. And that's because in the beginning, before the rewards and benefits are truly known so that they become the source of motivation, you'll sometimes just feel like you're going through the motions. But once you get into the habit of regular meditation, the benefits you get fuel your motivation.

Experts suggest that it takes about three or four weeks to turn a new activity into a habit. That means if you can motivate yourself for about the first month, it will get a whole lot easier.

By that point (if not before) you'll start looking forward to your meditation sessions.

You may find you get irritable if you don't get a chance to do them. And you'll never feel like your meditation session is taking the place of something else you'd rather do, because meditating will become THE thing you want to do (i.e., you'll place it above everything else).

All of this means your first task is to do whatever it takes to make sure you meditate regularly for about the first month. After that, it will be a natural part of your routine.

> *TIP: When you first start out, your enthusiasm will naturally be high. Everything is so new and exciting, so you probably can't wait to start meditating! And you're probably wondering why I'm even talking about motivation – after all, you can imagine yourself*

motivating every day for the rest of your life, right?

But here's the thing...

After a couple weeks the novelty will wear off. Meditation won't be as mysterious, new and exciting as it is today. While you'll be getting some benefit, you won't yet have received all the benefits we've talked about. And since you're still learning, you may at times feel frustration creeping up because you're not keeping your mind clear and calm.

Those couple weeks between when the "newness" wears off and before meditation becomes a habit is your danger period. This is the time when it's easiest to start skipping meditation sessions. But you need to fight the urge to do this. Otherwise, skipping your sessions will become the habit.

Let's now look at nine tips to help you find and maintain your motivation to meditate...

Tip #1: Make a list of your reasons for meditation.

We all meditate for different reasons. Some want to manage stress. Some want to become spiritually enlightened. Others do it for the physical and health benefits. And still others do it for all these reasons.

The first thing you need to do is clearly identify your personal reasons for meditating. What initially drew you to meditation? What benefits do you hope to achieve?

Don't just *think* about these benefits – go ahead and write them down.

Next: In order to turn these benefits into motivation, you need to be able to fully imagine yourself receiving the benefits. What's more, you need to find an emotional reason why you want these benefits – and then you need to imagine how you'll FEEL when you get those benefits.

For example, let's suppose one of your main reasons for meditating is to manage stress, lower your blood pressure and thus reduce your heart attack risk. Just thinking about those benefits is a mild motivator. But now imagine how you'll feel in when the doctor tells you that your blood pressure is normal. Now it becomes a much bigger motivation, doesn't it?

Likewise, you can do this with any other benefits you hope to achieve. If you want spiritual enlightenment, then think about how you'll feel as you get closer to your god. If you want calm and peace, then imagine how good it will feel to be able to unwind, de-stress and relax.

Now write down a few words describing what it will feel like to get all the benefits you desire. Then whenever you feel like skipping your planned meditation session, re-read this list and fully imagine yourself enjoying the benefits.

Tip #2: Stop yourself when you make excuses.

It's easy to rationalize. We say skipping "just one" meditation session won't hurt anything. In truth, it probably WON'T hurt to skip a session every now and then. But the problem is this: If you're just starting out, then skipping one session can lead to skipping another session... and so on.

So what you need to do is put a stop to these rationalizations where you talk yourself into skipping a session. The first step is to simply recognize yourself doing it... and then tell yourself the TRUTH.

Let's suppose you catch yourself saying, "I'm going to skip meditating this morning. I'll do it tonight instead."

Ask yourself: Is that the truth? Are you being honest with yourself?

If you're not sure whether you're being honest with yourself, imagine that you were making a promise to someone else. Imagine your mother asked you to do something for her one morning.

Could you honestly tell her that you couldn't do it at the originally planned time, but that you'll do it in the evening instead?

That is, are you honestly planning on REALLY doing it in the evening – or are you just putting off to the evening, but you'll probably skip it then too?

See, sometimes we tell ourselves we'll skip our planned meditation session in the morning because we can do it in the evening instead. But if we're honest with ourselves, we know we won't have time in the evening. There's work, grocery shopping, picking the kids up from daycare, fixing dinner, cleaning up after dinner, calling a friend for their birthday, giving the kids a bath... and on and on!

In sum: Whenever you catch yourself making excuses as to why you're not going to do your meditation session, confront yourself. Find out if you're being truthful. Because just as you seek to be truthful in your dealings with others, you deserve to be truthful with yourself, too.

Tip #3: Keep a meditation journal.

Another way to keep yourself motivated is to keep a meditation journal. Your meditation journal should include two things:

1. *Your scheduled meditation sessions*. Even if you plan to meditate every day at exactly the same time, you should draw up a weekly schedule and put it in writing. In addition, you need to be specific, by noting the exact days and times you plan to meditate. If you just say you'll meditate

"every day" (or using some other vague description), it's much easier for you to skip a session since it really wasn't official anyway.

TIP: Just the act of putting it in writing serves to help seal up your commitment. It's kind of like making a contract with yourself. However, if you find putting your schedule in writing doesn't help you much, then DO draw up a "contract" with yourself. List all the times you intend to meditate. Then sign it like you would a contract. For extra motivation, have a witness sign it as well.

2. *Thoughts and other notes about your completed meditation sessions.* The second thing you should put in your journal are notes about your completed meditation sessions. You may keep this as a log of how long you meditated, how well you thought the session went, how you felt before and after, etc.

Again, this is a simple psychological motivator. When you know you have to record your meditation session in a journal, you're much more likely to do it. That's because we all hate to have the words "skipped" or "missed session" in our logs, as it serves as a reminder of us deliberately skipping out on meditating. To avoid that sort of psychological discomfort, we instead do the session so we can log it.

Tip #4: Create a ritual.

Let me ask you a question…

Have you ever started making dinner… and suddenly you found yourself extremely hungry? Just moments before you didn't feel particularly hungry. And yet now that you're cutting the vegetables and preparing your meal, your stomach is growling.

The reason this happens is because the ritual of preparing dinner acts as a psychological trigger.

You've been "trained" (conditioned) to expect to eat soon after you start making dinner. So when you start preparing the meal, the conditioned reflex kicks in and your body prepares to eat. You're probably seen conditioned reflexes in another situations. For example, perhaps a certain candle scent makes you feel romantic, simply because you've used it in a romantic situation before. Or a certain type of music makes you feel anxious because you've associated it with a scary movie.

As you've probably already guessed, you can use this conditioning to your advantage when you meditate. And the way to do that is to create some sort of ritual around your meditation sessions.

For example, you may start by slipping into your most comfortable outfit. Then you may choose to set the mood by lighting a candle, adjusting the blinds, turning off the lights, etc. Then perhaps you'll prepare the place you intend to sit, such as by adjusting the pillows on your recliner or taking out your meditation stool.

If you follow the same ritual every time before you meditate, soon the ritual itself will become associated with meditation. Even if you initially don't feel like meditating, just getting into your meditation outfit and preparing your space will increase your desire to meditate.

Tip #5: Just do it.

It's true that it's difficult to meditate when you really don't feel like doing it. You feel like you're going through the motions. And it's difficult to keep your focus.

Knowing this makes it all the more likely that, from time to time, we'll skip a session.

It's easy to tell yourself that since you don't feel like it, today isn't a good day to meditate. (Of course sometimes those days when we least feel like meditating are actually the days when we'd derive the most benefit!)

So what happens when you simply don't feel like it? Just do it anyway.

As mentioned just a moment ago, sometimes the mere act of preparing to meditate will put you in the mood. At other times, spending just five minutes in quiet solitude will change your attitude and make you open to this particular meditation session.

So even if you don't feel like it, tell yourself you'll meditate for five or ten minutes. Chances are, you'll be glad you did.

Tip #6: Meditate for short periods.

When you're just getting started with meditation, you may find it difficult to sit and focus for long periods of time. You may get uncomfortable (at least until you figure out the best position). Or you may just find it hard to keep your mind focused since it's used to chasing thoughts.

As such, the thought of doing a long meditation session likely sounds like a lot of work. You may be reluctant to do it. And that makes it pretty easy for you to make excuses as to why you don't need to meditate. Bam, just like that, you find yourself skipping meditation sessions.

Fortunately, this little motivation-killer is easy to fix: Just don't schedule long meditation sessions for yourself. It's much easier to sit down for a 15 minute session as opposed to thinking you should sit down for 45 minutes or more. (It's also easier to find the time for a short session, which also helps you develop the habit of regular meditation.)

TIP: While you may actually commit to meditating for about 15 minutes or so per day, ideally you should set more time aside. That way, if you find that you're having a particularly enjoyable session, you don't need to rip yourself away just because 15 minutes is up.

Tip #7: Try activity meditation.

Meditation is a good tool for pulling back from the chaos and stress of the world. However, when you're just starting out, you may find that the chaos and stress of the world KEEPS you from meditating. You lose the motivation to meditate because you're "too busy" (even though, ironically, it's during these "too busy" times that you'd greatly benefit).

Sometimes you even start feeling guilty for taking time for yourself to meditate. This happens even though rationally you know you NEED this time to yourself to de-stress and center yourself.

When you're so used to multi-tasking and being on the go, simply setting aside time to sit quietly seems... wasteful. (Even though it's truly valuable.)

So how can you alleviate these guilt feelings and the feeling like you need to multi-task?

Simple: By using activity meditation from time to time. That means you meditate while you're walking, gardening, eating or even doing household chores like dusting or doing the dishes.

Now, I'm not suggesting that you satisfy your need to multi-task by always engaging in some form of activity meditation. However, if you find yourself reluctant to do your meditation sessions because you feel like you need to be "doing" something, then give activity meditation a try – if only for a few sessions per week.

Later on, when you're in the habit of meditating regularly, you'll want to try the basic breath meditations.

Tip #8: Use tools like guided meditation scripts (recording).

As mentioned before, sometimes it's hard to get motivated to meditate when you feel distracted by the worries of the world. The idea of sitting quietly and clearing your mind doesn't even really seem possible.

That's where a guided meditation recording can help. Sometimes it's just easier to focus on someone telling you what steps to take during your meditation sessions (as opposed to trying to focus on your own inner monologue).

If you're just starting out, you'll also find guided meditation sessions useful because you don't need to think about what to do next. You won't find yourself wondering if you're breathing at the right pace or trying to remember what you're supposed to do next. Instead, all you have to do is focus on what the voice is telling you to do.

Tip #9: Find someone to hold you accountable.

Remember earlier when I said you could write a contract, sign it, and have at least one other person sign it as your witness? That's powerful, because we're much more likely to keep our promises when we get someone else involved. As such, finding someone to hold you accountable is an excellent way to keep yourself motivated during the "danger period."

There are a few different ways to approach this...

One way is to find a meditation partner. This may be someone you already know – someone who lives locally so that you can meet and meditate.

If you don't intend to actually meditate alongside this other person (as that can be distracting for some people), then you can even find someone online who's interested in talking with you about meditation and will help hold you accountable.

You may even get together (online, offline or on the phone) with an entire group of meditation enthusiasts. Group enthusiasm tends to be contagious. It's hard to feel unmotivated to meditate when you're with a group of people who are talking excitedly about their past and upcoming meditation sessions!

> *TIP: If you find a meditation partner, be sure that you don't turn this into a competition to see who's "better" at meditation. Find someone who, like you, will view this in a non-competitive manner because he or she realizes you're each on your own path.*

Alternatively, you can simply choose a friend, spouse or family member to hold you accountable. This person may or may not be interested in the topic of meditation – and that doesn't matter, as you won't actually be discussing your experience with this person. Instead, you're just looking for someone who will touch base with you on a daily basis to find out what your future meditation goals are and to see if you met today's goals.

You see, having someone call you daily is a strong motivator. Because you know this person is going to ask you if you meditated, you'll feel psychologically uncomfortable if you have to confess that you didn't do it. (And if you lie about it, you'll feel even worse!) So the only way for you to avoid this discomfort is to meditate.

TIP: Finding someone who's supportive is key. You don't want to choose someone who holds all the common misconceptions about meditation. If this person doesn't believe in what you're doing – or, worse yet, if they actually ridicule or belittle you – then you don't want this to be the person holding you accountable.

Instead, find someone who's thrilled and enthusiastic when you tell them you've taken up meditation. Find someone who generally cares for you and is supportive about your goals.

Reflect

You just learned that sometimes it's hard to meditate regularly, especially in the period after your initial enthusiasm has waned, but before meditating is a habit. However, you also discovered nine ways to keep you motivated.

If you keep meditating for about a month, you'll find that meditation becomes a habit – and soon you'll eagerly look forward to each session!

Now let's turn our attention to meditation preparations...

Preparing to Meditate

Earlier in the book we briefly touched on the importance of choosing a quiet place, comfortable clothing and a good time to meditate.

Let's examine these issues (and others) in a little more detail...

Setting Aside Time to Meditate

As you've already discovered, simply saying "I'll meditate every day" isn't good enough. If you don't schedule a specific time, it's too easy to schedule all sorts of other activities right over your meditation time.

That's why you need to schedule meditation just like you schedule anything else. Just as you know exactly what time to go to work, or to pick up the kids or to go to the dentist for an appointment, you should also set aside a specific time for meditation. Write it down on your calendar (in ink). And make sure everyone else in your household is aware of when you plan to meditate.

Indeed, that last part is important. Even if you set aside to meditate, your meditation session can quickly be gobbled up by the interruptions from your family or others living in your home. That's why you need to ask them to leave you uninterrupted during your meditation session. And whenever possible, schedule your meditation session when everyone else is either asleep or away from home.

TIP: Sometimes it's difficult to schedule a meditation session at a time when everyone else is away from the house. One way to keep the interruptions to a minimum is to ask your family members to meditate with you (if that's not distracting to you).

When you're scheduling your meditation session, there are two things you need to keep in mind:

1) Choose a time when you're likely to be motivated to meditate. If you're in tune with your body, then you already know there are times of the day when you're not motivated to do much of anything. You should avoid scheduling your meditation sessions for those times.

For example, you may decide that the best time for you to set

aside some quiet time is first thing in the morning before everyone is awake. Further, you may like the idea of calming and grounding yourself before the rush of the day begins.
But here's the thing: That idea is only going to work if you're a morning person.

You see, if you're one of those people who hit the snooze button repeatedly and need several cups of tea or coffee just to get going in the morning, then a morning meditation session might not be your best option. It's entirely too easy to simply hit the alarm clock "snooze" button so you can grab an extra 30 minutes of sleep.

On the other hand, you may spring out of bed in the morning, but you find your energy and focus waning in the later parts of the day. In that case, an evening session may be out of the question... especially if you tend to have family obligations right up until bedtime.

In addition (as mentioned before), you'll want to shy away from high stress times. This is especially true when you're just starting out with meditation, as it can be hard to hold your focus when you clearly have some other pressing matter on your mind.

Bottom line: Everyone is different. So the point is, schedule a time that you believe works best for you.

2) *Set aside enough time to meditate*.

The second thing you need to keep in mind is that you need to schedule enough time for your session. While you can get benefit from just 15 minutes or so of meditation per day, whenever possible you should set aside more time. That way, you can officially say you'll meditate for 15 minutes – but if you want to meditate longer, you can since you've set aside extra time (and you won't feel rushed).

Not only should you set aside enough time, ideally you want to choose a non-rushed block of time. If you schedule in a fast 15 minutes right before you need to rush off to work, then you'll probably be very mindful of what time is it (and perhaps you'll spend your session worrying about getting to work on time).

One way to avoid this is to use a timer – that way you can focus on your meditation as opposed to sneaking peeks at your watch.

Some people use kitchen timers, alarm clocks and similar. However, these can be extremely jarring, thus pulling you out of your tranquil headspace. You may even start "bracing yourself" when you think the alarm is about to go off. In addition, many timers (such as kitchen timers) have a "tick tick" sound that can be distracting.

The solution? Use a specially designed meditation timer. These timers gently inform you of the start and the end of your sessions with a gentle, non-jarring sound.

Selecting a Quiet Place to Meditate

While some people (especially advanced practitioners) are able to meditate anywhere, initially you'll want to choose a place that's calm, quiet and relaxing to you.

For example, some people take a few minutes in the middle of the day to meditate at work. They'll often just shut their door and meditate for 15 minutes at their desks.

However, if you have a high-stress job, or if you're likely to be interrupted by co-workers or the phone, then this isn't a good idea. That's because even if you're not interrupted and even if the phone doesn't actually ring, you'll still likely be "on edge" because you're *expecting* these distractions. And further, it's hard to calm your mind in a place that you've already associated with chaos and stress.

> *TIP: If your company offers "sleep pods," take advantage of those for your meditation sessions.*

If you're meditating in the middle of the day, and if you associate your office building with high stress, then find someplace else to meditate. It may be in a nearby park, at a library, or some other quiet corner of a building.

If you meditate at home, then clear out some quiet corner and make it your "meditation corner." Obviously, you don't need a huge space – but you shouldn't feel cramped or feel like there's a lot of clutter in your meditation space.

TIP: You also don't need to get fancy equipment for your meditation room if you don't want to. You can buy a special meditation chair or stool if it suits you. If you intend to meditate on the floor, you may choose to buy meditation pillows or mats. But again, these are just options. You can just as well meditate in a comfortable chair, on a bed or even on the floor or on a regular pillow. The key is to do what makes you feel comfortable.

Ideally, this should be a space that you can claim entirely as your own. That way you can decorate it in a way that's pleasing to you, without having to worry about someone else throwing your meditation stool or pillows aside and creating clutter in your space. In addition, you won't have scheduling issues if your meditation space is yours alone.

Also, the same applies here as mentioned above. Namely, this should be a relatively stress-free corner of your home. You don't want to use the same corner or your house to meditate as you do to pay your bills. As you've already discovered, associations and conditioning count, which is why you want to associate your space with calm and quiet.

You can of course meditate outdoors as well. Unless you plan on doing a mindfulness meditation where you focus on what it feels like to be outdoors, don't go outside when the weather isn't mild. Otherwise, you're likely to find yourself thinking about how cold it is, how hot it is, how rainy it is, how windy it is, etc. If you're meditating on a sunny day, try to choose a shady spot.

When choosing a spot outdoors, be mindful of other possible distractions. For example, will you hear dogs barking in your chosen spot? Are there unpleasant odors wafting over to your chosen spot? Will mosquitoes or chiggers or other insects sting and bite you while you're meditating?

Be sure to follow your gut. Sometimes you may choose a space that seems like it would be the ideal space to meditate, yet your gut is telling you differently. Then for whatever reason, you just can't focus in that space. As such, you may need to experiment by trying out different locations to find the best one for you.

Creating the Mood

As mentioned before, you can create rituals to help you get in the mood to meditate. Even during those times when you're motivated to meditate, performing your ritual can help by calming you – even before you sit down!

Setting the mood starts by going to your meditation space. You may arrange your seating area, pull the curtains or shut the blinds and dim the lights. You may also choose to light incense or an aroma candle, being careful to choose a scent that you find relaxing. You may prepare your guiding meditation recording and perhaps a focal object (like a candle). And you'll set your meditation timer.

TIP: While some forms of meditation work best when you're in a space that's as quiet as possible, there may be times when you instead choose to play other sounds in the background. This can be soothing at any time. But you may find it particularly soothing to play a background noise if it helps to mask some other distracting noise that you'd rather not hear.

For example, you may choose a nature sounds recording, such as the sound of a waterfall, the wind rustling through the trees or waves lapping at the shore. Or perhaps you'd rather just mask the background entirely by using a white noise (such as a fan or static on the radio).

Finally, you'll want to slip into your comfortable clothing...

Choosing Comfortable Clothing

Finally, the last major preparation you need to make is to choose your meditation clothing.

Here again you can purchase clothing designed especially for meditation. However, if you feel relaxed, comfortable and calm in the clothing you already own, then you may certainly meditate in your existing clothing.

TIP: The advantage of purchasing new clothing just for your meditation sessions is that slipping into those clothes helps calm you (as it's part of your meditation ritual).

That's because it's much easier to purchase new clothing to include as part of your ritual, as opposed to trying to make new associations with old clothing. For example, if you're meditating in the same clothing you use to play sports, you may find yourself getting "fired up" as opposed to getting calm!

Here are a few tips to keep in mind as you choose your meditation clothing:

- *Choose loose clothing.* It's hard to meditate if your clothing is digging into your skin, which is why it's sometimes difficult to meditate in jeans and similar tight clothing.

If you are meditating at work or at some other time when you can't completely change clothes, then be sure to loosen your clothing. That means loosening your belt and tie, unbuttoning the top button of your shirt, taking off your shoes, etc.

If you're doing an activity meditation such as a walking meditation, then be sure to choose comfortable that moves freely with you. If you expect to get warm during the activity, choose clothing that helps wick away the moisture so that you stay comfortable. For example, choose hiking socks that are designed to keep your feet dry and comfortable, no matter what the temperature is.

Pay particular attention to your shoes if you're doing a walking meditation (or even if you're just walking or hiking to your chosen meditation spot). You want to choose shoes that are comfortable, worn-in and not prone to giving you blisters.

- *Opt for clothing that makes you comfortable.* You want to choose clothing that feels good against the skin and is breathable, such as silk or cotton.

That's because you don't want to be thinking about how "scratchy" or stiff your clothing is while you meditate.

In addition, be aware of features on your clothing that might distract you, such as the tag of your shirt or an unusual seam in the clothing.

- *Select the right clothing for your environment.* Finally, be sure to select clothing that's appropriate for the place you're meditating. If you're meditating outside, be sure to dress for the weather.

But even if you're meditating inside, be aware that sitting still and meditating for a period of time can cause your body temperature to drop slightly so that you may feel chilled. Thus it's a good idea to wear long sleeves or to set the thermostat to account for this drop in body temperature.

Reflect

Now that you've prepared to meditate, it's time to start your session…

Learning the Basics of Meditation

You're all ready to meditate. You've set aside enough time, set the right mood and chosen comfortable clothing. Now it's time to talk about the basics, including position, focus and breathing.

Choosing Your Position

If you recall, previously I mentioned that certain postures developed in part due to the practitioners' natural preferences. This is particularly true of those cross-legged positions (such as the half lotus) that you likely associate with those who meditate. That position became popular because it was a natural way of sitting for those who developed it – not necessarily because it is the "best" way to position yourself.

This means that the key to choosing a position is to choose something that's comfortable for you! This could be sitting, standing, kneeling, laying down … or even walking (as is the case with activity/walking meditation). If you get uncomfortable, then use another position. You want to focus on your meditation, NOT on the fact that your leg is falling asleep or getting a cramp. ☺

TIP: Regardless of what position you choose, be sure that it's one that allows you to breathe easily. If you're sitting, sit up straight so you can take deep, full breaths.

While you're position must be comfortable so that you can relax, it must also allow you to remain alert. In other words, you want

> *to be comfortable – but you don't want to fall asleep!*

You may need to experiment with different positions to see what works best for you. Below you'll find common sitting, standing, lying and activity positions that you can try – or create your own position.

> *TIP: If you're restless and find it difficult to sit still (at least initially), don't worry – you'll get better with practice. However, some people have found that studying Hatha Yoga – the yoga of positions – to be beneficial to their meditation postures.*

Sitting Positions

There are many sitting positions you can assume – some on the floor, some on a chair, some on a stool. Here are a few of the most common:

- *Floor: Cross-legged.* This is a simple position (the same position small children tend to get in naturally when they're sitting on the floor), and thus it generally doesn't require much flexibility on your part. One reason to choose this position is because it's keeps you fairly stable, which means you can focus on your meditation rather than worrying about whether you're going to fall over.

- *Floor: Seiza position.* The seiza position is where you're on your knees, feet and calves pointing behind you, and your buttocks are resting on the backs of your calves. To take the pressure of your legs, you can insert a pillow between your buttocks and the back of your calves. You can also purchase a seiza bench to sit on.

- *Floor: Kneeling.* Here you are in a kneeling position similar to the seiza position, except that you're not resting on your own legs. You may, however, lean forward and rest on something in front of you. (Think of a typical Christian praying position here.)

- *Floor: Half lotus position.* This is a more advanced posture since it requires a degree more of flexibility. Due to it's asymmetrical nature, it also requires you to balance your body.

Here's what it looks like…

You start off in a regular cross-legged position. Then put your left foot to rest on your right thigh (or vice versa). The other leg should remain tucked under. Be sure to keep your spine straight.

- *Floor: Full lotus position.* This is one of the more common positions you see, in part because it's considered one of the most stable positions. However, it does require you to develop some flexibility.

As you might suspect, the difference between

the full lotus and the half lotus is that both of your feet/ankles are resting on your opposite thighs. So you start off by sitting in the cross-legged position. Then put your left foot on your right thigh and put your right foot on your left thigh. The bottoms of your feet will be pointed towards you and slightly upward. Be sure to keep your spine straight.

- *Floor: Burmese position.* This is similar to the regular cross-legged position, except that it's more tightly controlled. That's because your legs, feet and even your knees should be in a straight line, resting flat on the floor.

Tip: Your ankles will be pointing straight up the center or your body. You may even rest your hands on your ankles.

- *Chair: Erect position.* Any type of chair will do, as long as you're comfortable. If you're sitting upright, then place your feet flat on the floor, as that will help you stay straight so you can breathe deeply. You may also place a small pillow behind you for lumbar support.

  Alternatively, if you're sitting on a large chair, couch or even on a bed, you can use some of the kneeling or cross-legged positions described above.

- *Chair: Reclined position.* As long as you are comfortable and can breathe deeply, you don't necessarily need to sit ramrod straight in a chair. Instead, you may opt to sit in a recliner so that you can recline back. You may even choose to recline back far enough so that you're essentially lying down (which we'll talk about shortly).

- *Chair or floor: The position of your choosing.* As mentioned, you don't necessarily have to choose a posture talked about above. Instead, you can use a comfortable position of your choosing.

For example, you may prefer to sit against a wall with your legs in front of you but bent at the knees and your feet flat on the floor. Or perhaps you prefer to have one leg tucked under you and one stretched out directly in front of you. The choice is yours.

What should you do with your hands in these positions?

Again, comfort is key, so choose a hand position that seems natural and comfortable to you.

Some people like to rest their hands at their sides. Some use their hands for the Yoni Mudra position (described earlier in the book). Some choose to rest their hands on their knees, palms up... and some prefer palms down.

Still others prefer the "cosmic mudra" hand position. To use this position, put your hands in front of you, both palms up. Lay one hand on top of the other, so that the fingers of the bottom hand come very close to the base of your thumb. Then put the tips of your thumbs together. This position creates an oblong circle, formed by your hands and thumbs.

What should you do with your eyes?

What you do with your eyes largely depends on what type of meditation you're doing.

Most times, it works best to close your eyes. That way your brain doesn't have to process the visual information that's coming in. You may also use a your fingers to close your eyes (the Yoni Mudra meditation position), or even use an eye mask if you prefer.

A second possibility is to keep your eyes open, but out of focus. Your eyes are open, but you're not really seeing anything. This eye position is of course the choice position when you're doing a walking meditation.

Finally, the third method is to choose an object to focus on. This is where you're doing a concentration meditation, with your focus centered on an object rather than your breathing (or anything else). The object you choose is up to you. You may choose to look at a candle flame, a photograph, a painting, a statue or anything else.

Lying Positions

Many people prefer lying positions as opposed to the more common sitting positions. This is particularly true when you're doing certain meditations that call for you to lie down, such as the death meditation.

Below I've described some of the most popular lying position. As usual, you can choose one from the list below or create your own (such as a half-reclined position in a chair).

> *NOTE: You need to choose a position that makes you comfortable yet alert. That is, you don't want to fall asleep while you're doing this.*

- *Lying flat, palms up.* Here you are stretched out flat with your legs slightly apart. In this position your arms are next to you, palms up. (This is important if you're doing certain energy meditations, as the palms up meditation helps you absorb the energy.

- *Lying flat, palms down.* This is the same stretched-out position as described above. However, here your palms are down on the ground.

- *Lying position, knees up, arms at side.* Here you lie flat on your back, knees bent so that your feet are flat on the floor or ground. Your knees and legs should be apart slightly. Your arms should rest at your side in either the palms up or palms down position.

- *Lying position, knees up, arms on body.* This

is the same body position as described above, with your knees up. The only difference that instead of resting your arms at your sides, you lay them on your body.

Generally, the most comfortable position is to put your hands on your stomach. This position allows you to be mindful of the way your breath moves your stomach. Alternatively, you can rest your hands on your chest. You may even cross your hands over your chest.

- *Lying position, legs crossed.* Here you cross your legs as if you were sitting, but then you lie down. Your arms can either be at your side (palms up or palms down) or on your body.

- *Corpse position*. This is where you lie down flat, legs straight out in front of you, feet slightly apart, arms on body. Again, you can put your hands on your stomach, on your chest, or you can cross your arms over your body.

While variations of lying on the back are the most common forms of lying meditation, you may of course choose any position that's comfortable for you. Just be sure that you can breathe deeply.

For example, you may lie on your side. If you do this, keep your back straight so its easy to breath. Also, you may find it comfortable to put a small pillow between your knees (some find it comfortable to put one between their ankles as well).

Another possibility is to lie down flat on your stomach with your legs stretched out behind you. Cross your arms on the floor and rest your forehead on your hands. Alternatively, if you have a massage table, then you can rest your arms at your side and rest your forehead in the headrest of the massage table.

The advantage of this particular position is that you tend to automatically breathe better since you'll be using your diaphragm. You'll learn more about diaphragm breathing just a bit later in this book.

Standing Positions

Some people prefer to stand while they meditate, often

because standing grounds you and your energy.

Here are two of the most common variations on this position:

- *Wu Ji position.* Here you stand with your arms at your sides, your feet about shoulder width apart. Your knees are slightly bent. Your head is up.

  One popular meditation in this position is similar to the body scan meditation, except that you start at the top of your head and move down. As you move down, you imagine the tension draining from your body.

- *Hands on stomach.* Here you stand in a

relaxed stance, feet about shoulder width apart. The difference is that one or both hands are on your stomach. You can then focus on the way your breath pushes your hand (or hands) in and out.

Activity Positions

Obviously, the position you use for your activity meditation largely depends on what activity you're doing. For example, it's common for people to meditate while they're doing yoga, Tai Chi, exercise or even chores.

However, since the walking meditation is one of the most common forms of activity meditation, we'll look at four different ways you can do your walk:

- *Walking in a line.* Here you choose a place to walk which is about 15 to 20 paces long. Then you walk back and forth on this straight line, keeping your eyes just beyond your feet. You can do this either inside or outside.

- *Walking in a circle.* Instead of walking in a straight line, you can instead choose to walk in a circle. Choose a circumference that's comfortable for you. Again, you can do this either inside or outside.

- *Walking in nature.* Instead of choosing a line or circle, you may instead choose to simply walk around your neighborhood, walk in a park, walk in the woods, walk in the mountains, etc. You may even do a short walking meditation when you're walking from a parking lot to your office.

- *Combination walking then sitting.* Some people prefer to start their meditation sessions by walking for about five or ten minutes, at which time they sit down and continue meditating. Try this for yourself and see if it helps clear your mind.

Now that you've chosen your position, let's move on to one of the most important parts of meditation: Breathing.

Breathing Correctly: The Power of Breath

In meditation, breathing is everything. Indeed, without breath, there is no meditation (which is why so many meditative practices focus on breath awareness and mindfulness). Some people have suggested that breath is the bridge between the body and the mind.

TIP: The power of breath has long been recognized by humans. Hindus refer to "prana," which is the life force (energy) we take in with each breath. While prana is not the breath itself, how we breathe helps us channel our prana.

Think of it this way…

Your body instinctively knows how to balance. When you move from a sitting to an upright position, it makes fine adjustments to your muscles so that you can do this movement smoothly and easily.

Now think about a new balancing experience, such as the first time you ever put on a pair of inline skates, roller skates or even ice skates. You sat in a chair, lacing them up, and then rose up out of that chair.

You had performed this action of rising up out of your chair to stand on your feet countless times before. Your body usually instinctively knew exactly what to do as you went from a sitting to standing position. You probably had never even thought about how your body does this since it's an automatic process.

But now that you had these skates on your feet, you became very aware of your need to keep your body balanced. You became keenly aware of what your muscles were doing in your legs, torso and arms in order to keep you upright. You even made conscious and voluntary adjustments, such as sticking your arms out for balance or perhaps grabbing onto an stable object. And you learned how to keep your balance simply by being very aware of your body.

Likewise, meditation breathing is learned through conscious awareness. Whereas you mainly breathe without even thinking of it (in much the same way you keep your balance), meditation breathing requires focus and awareness (just like the focus you use to learn how to skate).

This section will show you how to develop that conscious awareness…

How Do You Breathe?

Normally you breathe on autopilot. That means that you don't have to remind yourself to breathe. You don't have to tell yourself all through the day to "breathe in, breathe out." And you're not kept up at night reminding yourself to breathe. Instead, your brain works in tandem with your body so that you automatically pull air in and out of your lungs and use the oxygen in this air for vital processes in the body.

Normally, we're not even aware of our breathing. The only times we tend to consciously become aware of how we breathe is when something happens to change our normal breathing rate.

For example:

- We notice our hard breathing after a long run.

- We notice our breathing when we enter an environment with different air then we're used to, such as the warm, moist air of a Finnish sauna… or the cool, crisp air that freezes our nostrils on a January morning.

- And we certainly notice when we can't breathe, such as when we're swimming and we've misjudged just how far away the surface of the water is.

You may have also noticed your breathing changing in response to your emotions. Think back to a time when you were scared of some imminent danger that was right in front of you. Perhaps it was a snarling, menacing dog. Maybe you were afraid of someone following you on a darkened street. Or perhaps you just remember back to a time when you went through a haunted house when you were a child.

Do you remember what it felt like? Your heart rate quickened, you felt fear rising up in you, and you started breathing shallow yet faster.

This response is part of the "old brain" flight or fight response. Your body is basically gearing up for you to engage in a major physical activity.

For example, ancient man may have faced dangers, such as being cornered by a tiger or other wildlife. His flight or fight response caused a surge of adrenaline and prepared his body to either fight that tiger or run away as fast as possible.

As mentioned a moment ago, you've likely felt that same automatic response rise up in your body as the result of impending danger (or at least perceived danger).

Now here's the thing: Most of us don't live in a world where physical danger lurks around every corner. Instead, we have our modern day stressors, such as a high-pressure job. While our body isn't facing actual physical danger, it nonetheless reacts in much the same way as fight or flight response – and that means many people are living in a near-constant state of being "on edge" due to stress.

This stress results in many of the same signs, such as shallow breathing.

Think back to a time when you've felt stress and you'll see it's true. A non-physical situation that provokes anxiety – like the nerves you feel before giving a public speech or sitting for a job interview – usually result in an increased heart rate, sweaty palms, dry mouth and altered breathing.

Now consider how many people are stressed out and anxious on a daily basis by the demands of their family and job (or lack thereof), and there should be no doubt that we have plenty of people walking around who are nearly constantly breathing in "stress mode." That is, they are breathing using short, shallow breaths.

Here's why this is important to our study of meditation...

Just as how you feel can affect your breathing (e.g., if you're scared or stressed, you'll take shallow breaths), how you breathe can affect how you feel.

You can prove this quickly to yourself right now. Take several fast, shallow breaths for the next minute or two. Be mindful of how you feel as you breathe in this manner.

It really doesn't feel that good, does it? That's because we've associated that sort of breathing with stressful or dangerous situations. So simply breathing as if we're anxious can cause the anxious feelings to rise up inside of us!

Now I want you to reverse those feelings. Take another minute or two right now to breathe deeply and slowly. Savor each breath, being mindful of how it feels.

What a change! That feels good, doesn't it? It calms and relaxes you.

That's because deep, slow breathing is associated with being calm and relaxed. So just the act of breathing in that manner helps to calm us (even if we felt stressed before we started breathing like that).

Now you're starting to see the importance of breath and breath awareness in meditation. You see, our normal automatic breathing is nothing like the meditative breathing.

Normally, we take in pretty shallow breaths, even if we aren't stressed. And when we are stressed, our breathing becomes even more shallow and fast. This fast, shallow breathing causes us to feel worse, which results in even poorer breathing. And the vicious cycle continues.

On the flip side, meditation breathing is slow, deep and deliberate. We savor each breath as if we'd never breathed in such pure oxygen before (or as if we never expect to again). We calm our minds and bodies simply because we're very aware of and controlling our breathing.

Breath Awareness

You just discovered how breathing can calm you and why breath awareness is so important. Now in this section you'll learn more about breath awareness as well as different breathing techniques used in meditation.

Breathing with Your Diaphragm

If you've studied yoga, meditation or even singing before, then you're probably well aware that most people breathe "wrong." Just ask most people to take a deep breath, and then pull their shoulders up and puff out their chest. This is incorrect, as that indicates the person isn't breathing using their diaphragm.

The diaphragm is a muscle that lies across your rib cage. When you breathe using your diaphragm, your chest won't expand. Instead, your diaphragm pulls down slightly on the lungs, which allows them to draw in air. As such, you'll see your ribs push outward.

> *TIP: Some people say that as long as your chest remains still and your lower abdomen (belly) moves out, then you're breathing correctly. Indeed, this is an improvement over shallow chest breathing.*
>
> *However, an even better way to do it is to make sure your belly and your chest remain fairly still, and instead get the movement right over your upper abdomen, (below the breast bone). Doing so results in even deeper, more relaxing breathing.*

Learning diaphragm breathing takes practice, especially since most people naturally breathe without properly using the diaphragm. Here's how you can learn how to breathe properly.

Step 1: Get into a comfortable position. Some people prefer to sit, while others feel they can do this exercise better lying on their back.

Step 2: Put one hand on your chest and one hand on your belly.

Step 3: Now start breathing in deeply and slowly, noticing as you do so whether your chest or lower abdomen are moving. If they are, focus on breathing so that you detect movement only in the upper abdomen.

If you've discovered that you aren't naturally breathing using your diaphragm (and you probably aren't), then you should perform this simple exercise several times throughout the day.

For example, perform it before you get out of bed in the morning, when you're sitting in traffic on your way to work, at the office, back at home and last thing at night. Whenever you feel stressed, you may also perform this exercise to help calm you and to make sure you're breathing properly. And certainly when you're meditating you should be sure that you're breathing using your diaphragm and not your chest.

Becoming Aware of Your Breath

As you already know, becoming aware of your breath is part of many meditation practices. In some cases, you'll focus on how your breath feels. Other techniques have you counting your breaths. We'll get to some of these specific breathing techniques in just a moment. But first, I'd like to take you through an exercise that will enhance your meditation sessions by helping you become more aware of your breathing and how it affects you.

You can use this exercise independently since it is a meditation technique (where you become mindful of your breathing).

Or you can simply do the exercise from time to time to increase your awareness of how you breathe. (Doing so will help you breathe correctly when you're practicing other forms of meditation that don't keep you so focused on your breath.)

Here's how to do it…

Start in a position that's comfortable for you, either sitting or lying down. Just be sure that you sit with your back straight so that you can freely breathe (and your abdomen can flare out). Then place your hands on your chest and abdomen so that you can check how they're moving as you breathe.

Now start breathing in and out deeply. Generally, you draw in a breath through your nose and exhale the breath through your mouth.

Also, your exhalations should be roughly twice as long as your inhalations – as long as that's comfortable breathing rate for you. If you prefer, you may count to draw out your inhalations and exhalations. So for example, slowly count to four as you draw in a breath... and then count to eight as you exhale.

> *TIP: Take a moment to become aware of how you're breathing. That is, make sure that you're breathing using diaphragm as opposed to pushing*

your chest or lower abdomen out. Make any corrections if necessary.

Now pay attention to how you're breathing. As mentioned elsewhere in this book, imagine if you're taking your last few breaths of the purest air you've ever experienced. How would you take those breaths? How would you savor each breath? In what ways would you breathe more deeply, longer and more deliberately?

Whatever your answers to those questions, that's how you should be breathing as you perform this meditation exercise.

Next, start paying attention to your breath at the location of your nose, mouth and lips. Feel as it draws into your nostrils and downward. Pay attention to the sensation as you exhale and your breath runs through your mouth and dances lightly across your lips. Spend a few minutes focusing on your breath at this point on your body.

Take a moment and imagine pulling in clean, pure air. Imagine that air traveling down towards your lungs. Then as you exhale, imagine yourself expelling toxins and waste from the body.

> *TIP: To turn this into a more meaningful visualization, you may even imagine yourself pulling in healing white or yellow light (whatever you find soothing).*

Now focus your attention on your breath as it moves down to your lungs. Become aware of your lungs expanding as you draw in a deep breath. Feel as your lungs contract again as you exhale. Spend a few minutes focusing your attention on your breath at the point of your lungs.

Next, pay attention to the subtle movements of your body as you draw in a deep breath and then exhale it. Can you feel your back move slightly as your lungs expand? Can you feel the movement inside of your chest? Become aware of how your rib cage expands, and any movements you feel in your abdomen.

Now move your attention to your diaphragm muscle (which lies across your lower rib cage). Feel as it moves in response to your breath. Spend a few minutes focusing on your breath solely at this point in your body.

Next, think about your breath in relation to your entire body. Think of how each life-saving breath provides the needed oxygen that rushes to your brain and washes over you. Spend a few minutes focusing on your breath as it relates to your body.

If you're doing a regular meditative session, you can now just continue to breathe deeply (and correctly) while focusing on any part of the breathing process that you prefer. If you choose, you may do a breath counting meditation instead. Or alternatively, now that you're relaxed, you can start an entirely new meditation (such as a concept meditation).

However, if you're doing this exercise for the first time, then I suggest that you continue with the instructions below. That's because what follows will allow you to observe how subtle changes in the way you breathe affect you. And overall, this simple exercise will further raise your awareness of how you breathe, which means you'll start breathing better all the time (not just during your meditation sessions).

Let's continue...

Advanced Breath Awareness

Right now you should be breathing in through your nose and out through your mouth. Close your mouth so that you are only breathing through your nostrils. Continue taking deep breaths, with your exhalations being roughly twice as long as your inhalations.

Focus on your breath as it moves in and out through your nostrils. Think about how it feels as compared to moving your breath in through your nostrils and out through your mouth.

Now open your mouth again. This time, breathe entirely through your mouth. You may have a natural inclination to draw your breaths in through your nose, especially since you just spent the last several minutes practicing this. If need be, assume the Yoni Mudra position and pinch off your nostrils (and keep them pinched for a few minutes).

Once again, focus on your breath as it moves in and out through your mouth, over your tongue and across your lips. How does this feel different to you as compared to when you inhale through your nostrils and out through your mouth, or when you breathe entirely through your nose?

Next, it's time utilize both your nostrils and your mouth again. This time, breathe in through your mouth and out through your nostrils (i.e., do just the opposite of what you did during the basic breath awareness meditation). Breathe deeply, with the exhale being roughly twice as long as the inhale.

Focus on your breath in your mouth as you inhale, and focus

on how it feels as you exhale through your nose. How does this feel different than the other forms of breathing, such as the all mouth or all nose breathing?

Now return to the normal breathing where you inhale through the nostrils and exhale out through the mouth. Focus for a minute or two on deep breathing, counting to four on the inhale and counting to eight on the exhale.

Next, let's focus on what it feels like to change your rate of breathing. Try these variations, noting how the change makes you feel:

- Count to four as you inhale and immediately exhale while counting to eight. Focus on making your breathing smooth as you switch between inhaling and exhaling. Do not pause between the two.

- Count to four as you inhale, then hold your breath for five seconds. Then exhale slowly while counting to eight.
- Now reverse the inhalation and exhalation counts. Count to eight as you inhale. Then immediately exhale (without pause) and count to four. Notice how rushed your breath feels as you work to expel all the air you took in.

- Reverse the inhalation and exhalation with a pause. Now do the same thing as the above variation, in which you inhale for eight seconds and exhale for four seconds. This time, however, pause between the inhale and the exhale for five seconds.

Finally, do this...

Breathe in through your nostrils deeply and out through your mouth. This time, don't count anything. Instead, just focus on taking deep breaths that are comfortable for you. Make slight adjustments to your breathing until you find a rhythm that makes you feel calm, peaceful and comfortable.

Once you've found a breathing pattern that's deep yet comfortable, THEN count. But don't force a count (such as four or eight seconds). Instead, your job is to breathe deeply and count how many seconds you naturally inhale or exhale.

You may find that it's four seconds in and six seconds out. Or you may find it's five seconds in and seven seconds out. Once you determine that number, write it down so you don't forget it. When you're meditating, you'll want to always seek to reach that perfect breathing rate, so counting your inhalations and exhalations will help you get there.

-- END OF EXERCISE --

This breathing exercise is now over, and you certainly learned a lot about how your breath affects the way you feel. Now let's look at some of the other ways you can become more aware of your breath during meditation...

Learning Breathing Techniques

If you didn't realize when you first started reading this chapter just how important breath awareness is to your meditation, by now you're probably starting to get a pretty good idea.

And because it is so important (there is no meditation without proper breathing), we're spending a lot of time discussing how to breathe properly and become more aware of the power of breath.

In this section you'll discover still more breathing techniques to help you learn to become aware of your breathing, control your breathing, and harness its power...

Weighted-Abdomen Breathing Technique

You've already learned how to breathe using your diaphragm (as opposed to the more common, but shallow, "chest breathing" method). To further increase your awareness of diaphragmatic breathing, as well as to increase the strength of your diaphragm, you can try this simple weighted-abdomen technique.

All you have to do is create some sort of comfortable weight, perhaps by putting about 10 to 15 pounds of rice, sand or another similar substance into a bag. You want to have a substance in the bag that's malleable, so that it conforms to your body and doesn't slide off.

Next, simply lie down flat on your back, put the weight on your upper abdomen, and start breathing deeply. Because of the weight, you'll be very aware of whether you're using your diaphragm properly. As a nice bonus, you'll be strengthening this muscle.

Alternate Nostril Breathing Technique

As mentioned previously, some refer to the life force energy in your body as prana, and they say you can help control and regulate this energy by breathing correctly. However, breathing correctly goes beyond merely breathing using the diaphragm – it also means you need to learn how to balance your breaths.

Still others don't refer to prana directly, but they nonetheless advocate the importance of learning breath balance. Learning to balance one's breathing is directly related to "centering" oneself, calming the mind and otherwise relaxing. Thus it's useful to learn how to balance the breath.

Now here's the curious thing: Your body naturally regulates your breathing so that you only breathe out of one nostril at a time. Scientists suggest that you alternate between nostrils about every three hours.

You can discover this for yourself right now by closing your mouth, putting your fingers just below your nostrils and breathing deeply. Do you feel that? Air only comes out of one nostril as you exhale (and it only goes into one nostril as you inhale).

While this is perfectly natural, breathing with just one nostril does lead to an imbalance (and that may include you only engaging one side of the brain). If you can learn to breathe by alternating your nostrils, you'll feel calmer, more relaxed and enjoy a deeper meditation session.

Here's how to learn how to alternate nostrils. Note that this exercise can be done any time, any place. (Also note that you shouldn't do this exercise if you have a cold or other obstruction to nasal breathing, as you don't want to force yourself to breathe this way.)

Close your mouth and put your fingers on your nose, pinching off your right nostril. Now breathe in deeply and slowly through your left nostril, then exhale slowly through your nostril. Do this four or five times in a row.

Now switch sides. This time pinch off your left nostril to obstruct the passage of air. Now breathe deeply and slowly through your right nostril. Again, do this four or five times in a row.

You've just completed one round (or cycle). Now do another round by starting again from the beginning by pinching off your right nostril while breathing in and out deeply four or five times. Then switch and pinch off your left nostril to complete the round.

You can do this a few more times so that you do approximately three to five rounds each time you do the exercise. Do try to complete three to five rounds two or three times per day for a few days.

Once you are comfortable with physically controlling your breath by pinching off one of your nostrils, it's time to learn how to do it solely with your mind. First, determine which nostril is currently dominating. Then sit quietly for a few minutes, focusing on that nostril and how it feels to breathe out of that nostril.

After a few minutes, focus instead on your other nostril. Imagine yourself breathing freely and deeply through that nostril. With focused attention, you should be able to switch nostrils.

> *TIP: If you find it difficult to switch it solely using your mind, spend some more time practicing by*

pinching off nostrils. However, just before you pinch off a nostril, focus on breathing deeply and freely through the intended nostril. The pinch off the one you want blocked.

In other words, don't depend solely on the actual physical blocking off of your nostril with your fingers. You want to start incorporating mind control alongside the physical blocking. Doing so makes it much easier to eventually do it solely through mind control.

Do a few rounds where you practice taking four or five deep breaths before switching nostrils.

Walking Breath

Here's another technique that you can do any time that you're walking. You can do it as part of your walking meditation, or you can do it any time you're moving (even if you're just walking down a hall at work or walking through a parking lot).

Here you count how many steps you take for each inhalation and exhalation. Start off by walking at a normal pace and breathing normally. Then start counting how many paces you take to inhale... and how many paces you take to exhale.

As already know, the exhale is generally longer than the inhale. Thus, you'll likely take more paces on the exhale than you take on the inhale. For example, you may find that you take four footsteps as you inhale and six footsteps as you exhale.

Once you've discovered the most comfortable rhythm, keep

counting and walking, matching your paces to your breath. You may count out loud or silently, focusing your attention on the counting.

"The Bee" Technique

The Bee breathing technique – more formally known as Brahmari – gets its name from the fact that the noise you produce sounds much like the buzzing of a bee.

Start by sitting upright or lying flat – either way is fine, so long as you're not slouching or otherwise restricting your breathing. Close your mouth and put your lips together. Keep the back of your throat open. Now all you have to do is simply make the sound like the buzzing of bee, by exhaling and focusing on creating the vibration from back in your throat.

Ujjayi Breathing Technique

Here's a fairly common controlled breathing technique that's fairly simple. Because of the light, snore-like noise you make, it's sometimes called the "sounding breath" or even the "ocean breath."

The easiest way to get started is to first think about what people sound like when they're snoring. The reason they make this noise is because the epiglottis at the back of the throat is half closed, which restricts the airflow and creates the "rasping" sound.

Go ahead and try to make this sound yourself by moving the epiglottis in the back of your throat. Once you're able to do this so that you're making a snore-like sound, soften it. You don't want this to sound like a loud snore or other jarring noise. Rather, you want to make a soft, ocean-like whisper.

Once you're making this sound at the whisper level, breathe in and out deeply. Then focus your attention on the sound you're making.

Skull Shining Breath Technique

This is a breath technique that you can use to expel toxins and help center yourself before you begin meditating. Here's how it works…

Get into a position that is comfortable and allows you to breathe deeply and easily. Take a nice, deep (yet passive) inhalation. Then expel this breath out forcefully. Keep repeating the passive inhalation followed the forceful exhalation for about five or six breaths.

TIP: One variation is to inhale normally, then form your lips into a small circle (as if you were about to drink through a straw) and exhale forcefully.

Breath-Slowing Technique

If you listen closely to the breathing of someone who's deeply relaxed and perhaps asleep, you'll notice that he or she take long inhales and exhales. And as you've already discovered, simply learning to breathe more deeply will help calm, center and relax you.

So far, you've learned how to breathe more deeply. Now let's look at an exercise that can help you further stretch out the time between a full breath...

Start by lying down flat on your back, putting your hands where they are most comfortable for you. Begin by breathing deeply. If you find yourself pausing between breaths, eliminate that pause so that you are either constantly (yet slowly) inhaling or exhaling.

Initially you may find yourself doing an 8 to 12 second breath (with a smaller portion of that time going to the inhale and a significantly longer time spent exhaling). Now focus on slowing your breath down further so that you're only take three or four breaths per minute.

So far, this should be very comfortable and relaxing for you. Remember, you don't want to force anything.

NOTE: If you start feeling discomfort in any of the steps below, then go back to a place where you were comfortable and practice slowly stretching out the time it takes you to complete a breath.

And please note that attaining the upper levels will take weeks or even months of practice. In other words, this isn't something you learn how to do in one sitting!

Now focus on continuing to slow your breath down even further by making your breath inhalation and exhalation last 30 seconds. That means that you're taking two complete breaths per minute.

Once you are comfortably doing this, slow it down further. Make the exhalation/inhalation cycle last 45 seconds. Then increase it to a full minute so that you're taking just one full breath per minute.

This may take some practice to reach the 45 second and one-minute levels. Once you've reached these levels, you can start reaching even higher, by aiming for a 90 second breath.

Keep in mind, however, that this is an advanced technique. As such it may take you many months of practice (perhaps even a year) to reach this level. Be patient and keep practicing.

Breath-Mantra Meditation

Earlier we talked about how you can match your footsteps to your breath when you do a walking meditation. If you do a mantra meditation, you can match your breath to your mantra.

There are a few different ways to do this. If you're using a short mantra (such as a one syllable word or sound), then you may say your mantra on the inhale OR on the exhale. Do both and see which one is most comfortable for you.

If you have a multi-syllable or multi-word mantra, then you can say one part on the inhale and one part on the exhale.

> *TIP: Because your exhale is generally longer than your inhale, you may say the longer part of your mantra on the exhale. Again, do whatever seems the most natural and comfortable for you.*

For example, let's say you've chosen the mantra, "The Universe provides," you may say "the Universe" on the inhale, and then draw out the word "provides" on the exhale. Like this:

Inhale: The Universe...
Exhale: Prrrroooovvvviiideess

Also note: While you can say your mantra out loud (thus focusing on either the sound or the concept), you don't have to. Instead, you can think it silently while still matching it to your breath.

Reflect

Without proper breathing, there is no meditation. That's why you just discovered how to breathe correctly, control your breathing and harness its power through various breathing techniques and exercises.

Now let's turn our attention to another important component of meditation.

Namely: Focus.

Focusing Your Mind

Your mind is in a constant state of thought, even while you're asleep (hence your dreams). Thinking is automatic. But the problem is, we tend to chase our thoughts and even encourage them. And in doing so, this can lead to less desirable behaviors such as worry.

Because chasing your thoughts seems so natural, you probably hardly ever notice yourself doing it.

Maybe once in a while you'll realize you were thinking of something else while someone was talking... and thus you have to ask them to repeat what they said. Or sometime when you're reading you realize you've stared at the same page for five minutes and yet you don't have a clue what it says (because you were thinking of something else).

However, the times you'll most notice your thoughts barreling around your mind like a freight train is when you try to calm your mind through meditation. Suddenly the fact that you're chasing your thoughts becomes not just noticeable, but painfully obvious.

If you've already started meditating, then you know what I mean. And if you haven't yet sat down for your first meditation session, as soon as you do you'll understand all of this perfectly clear!

You see, it seems like it should be easy to quiet the mind. But as mentioned just moments ago, that's because we're not fully aware of how much thinking we do in any given moment.

So you sit down to meditate. You're looking forward to this session, this new experience. You decided to do a simple breath meditation where you focus on your breathing, perhaps even counting your breaths...

Then it happens. While it seems you've just begun, already you detect an intruding thought trying to break your concentration. Suddenly you find yourself wandering if you remembered to pay the cable bill...

And you wonder how much wood could a woodchuck chuck if a woodchuck could chuck wood...
☺

And you suddenly remember that you need to sign a permission slip for your child...

And you think you better leave extra time today when you go to pick up the kids, because you need to fill the car with gas...

And wow, are you ever feeling sleepy – you think maybe you should try to get to bed early tonight...

And you wonder if there's any chance of losing your job, even though you just survived the last round of layoffs. That thought sends a little surge of panic through you... at which point you suddenly remember you're supposed to be meditating, which means you shouldn't be thinking about all of this other stuff!

So you return to your counting and your breathing. But perhaps only a few minutes pass before your mind is running off like a pack of wild horses again.

Now let me say this: If you haven't yet sat for your first meditation session, it's not a matter of "if" the scenario I just described above will happen to you. It's a matter of how many times it will happen during each session.

As you start meditating, you'll find that there two types of distractions:

1. *Internal distractions.* These are the distractions described above, where your mind starts chasing thoughts. You could completely close off all your sensory perceptions, and you'd still have these distractions because your mind wants to focus on things other than your breath, mantra or other object of focus.

2. *External distractions.* These are the distractions happening outside of your mind. Some of them may be part of your body, such as the distraction you'll encounter when you realize your foot is falling

asleep. Other external distractions include the phone ringing, kids crying, the traffic on the street, the TV or radio, the sounds of people talking or yelling, road construction noises, rain (either on the window if you're inside, or on you if you're outside) and so on.

Obviously, you should work to decrease the external distractions whenever possible. That means choosing a quiet place to meditate, turning off your phones, shutting the windows to block out some of the street noise and so on. Fortunately, your ability to learn to ignore things like street noise and other distractions will grow with time.

The second types of distractions are those internal distractions. You overcome these by doing gently and persistently refocusing your mind to your breathing, to you counting or whatever type of object or concept you're focusing on.

Tamping Down the Perfectionist

Now, I know there are a few die-hard perfectionists reading this book. Maybe you're one of them. You want to do meditation "right" – and that includes calming your mind. So when your mind starts wandering, you get frustrated. Problem is, the more frustrated you get, the harder it is to calm your mind and refocus back to something else.

What can be even more frustrating to those who are just starting to meditate is the frequency with which it happens during a meditation session. You might set aside 15 or 20 minutes for meditation. And you might find yourself having to refocus 15 or 20 times (or about once or more per minute).

At first you'll gently refocus your mind, perhaps by focusing on a repetitive activity like counting. Then your mind wanders again, and you refocus again (still being gentle with yourself). It wonders repeatedly, and you gently refocus repeatedly.

After perhaps half a dozen times when it wanders, you start judging yourself. And maybe you even wondering if you're doing something wrong. But the fact that you're evaluating your performance means you're not focusing on your meditation.

Here's the thing...

Meditation is a skill like anything else, which means that it requires practice. When you were a toddler, you didn't one day just stand up and start walking perfectly. You needed to grab onto the furniture. You fell down a lot. Sometimes you had amazing, near-perfect bursts where you'd walk across a room – but then you'd fall down when you got to the other side.

This sort of thing didn't just happen when you were a child. Indeed, you had fits and starts and hours of practice for most any skill you've acquired:

- You didn't play a Beethoven piece within the first few months of taking piano lessons.

- When you learned how to drive a manual transmission car, you probably pushed the accelerator too much, made the gears grind, or stalled the car several times before you learned how to drive a stick shift smoothly.

- When you learned how to type on a keyboard,

you hunted and pecked at the keys, typing slowly, looking at your hands. With practice you became faster and more proficient.

See what I mean? You rarely do anything perfectly at first. Meditation is no different.

One more example...

Do you know how to juggle? If so, then you know that initially you spend more time dropping the balls then having them in the air. You throw the ball in your right hand. Then you throw the ball in your left hand. And by that time the first ball is already coming down, which you miss catching. Both balls hit the floor, so you patiently start over.

Meditation is no different. When you first start out, you may find that you spend more time with your mind wandering than you actually spend concentrating on your breath, mantra, concept or other object of focus. And that's ok.

With practice, you'll get better (although keep in mind that you shouldn't look at this as some sort of competition). Soon you'll notice that you're spending more and more time in deep focus. Eventually you'll come to a point where you spend most of your meditation sessions focusing, and/or you're able to lengthen your meditation sessions with ease.

Which brings us to the golden question...

What should you do when you find your mind wandering during meditation?

First things first: Don't be hard on yourself. Don't judge yourself harshly if you find it difficult to keep focused on your mantra, breathing or whatever else it is you're focusing on. You've spent your entire life chasing your thoughts, so it's unreasonable to expect that you'll be able to instantly control and focus them.

This is particularly important during your meditation session when you first notice your mind is wandering. After you notice this, your next thought may be something along the lines of, "oh dang! I can't keep my mind focused!" And if you do that, then you'll just keep chasing that thought and beating up on yourself.

Instead, what you need to do is simply acknowledge that yes, your mind is wandering. You may even feel pleased with yourself for noticing. Either way, you make this observation casually, without judgment. Then you gently nudge your mind back towards the object of your focus (your breath, counting, your mantra, a candle, a concept, etc).

The key here is that you acknowledge stray thoughts without judgment. One way to think of it is to imagine you're simply watching thoughts and images on TV. The stray thoughts are like the commercials. You need to push the "mute" button so they'll go away, thus allowing you to refocus on your object of focus.

Some people describe the experience of intrusive thoughts in terms of clouds. These clouds drift into your mind and obscure your focus. You acknowledge them and watch them drift gently away, thus bringing your object of focus back into full view. Again, you do so without judgment or emotion.

> *TIP: Meditating is not about "going blank" and*

not thinking. Instead, it's about controlling your thoughts by focusing on the object or concept of your choice. It's about not reacting to other stray thoughts.

Strengthening Your "Focus Muscle"

As touched on before, the reason our mind wants to continually wander during meditation is simply because its so used to chasing thoughts. During meditation, you're asking it to do something that you rarely if ever do otherwise. As such, it's going to take some practice to learn how to focus for longer periods of time.

Here's the thing…

Our minds are also rarely if ever living in the present moment. Just track your thoughts sometime (go ahead, let them wander and you can chase them), and you'll find that your mind is usually thinking about something from the past or something in the future – but rarely is it focused on the here and now.

For example, what are you thinking about as you read this book? If you're thinking about what you're reading (i.e., your mind isn't wandering away from the topic), then my guess is that you are thinking about one of two things:

> 1. You're thinking about how your past meditation sessions are similar or different to what I've described. Like for this particular session of the book, you're probably thinking about how your own mind has

wandered during a past meditation session.

If you're not thinking about your past meditation session, then here's my second guess:

2. You're thinking about a future meditation session. You're thinking about how you're going to incorporate this advice and these tips into your next meditation session. You probably can even imagine yourself sitting for a meditation session just a bit later today.

Now pull your eyes away from this book for about a minute or two. Let your thoughts run where they may. Keep track of what you think about.

(Go ahead and do it right now.)

.
.
.
.
.
.
.
.
.

Ok, you're back? What did you think about?

Maybe you were still thinking about meditation, so you thought of the two things mentioned above. Or maybe you started thinking about other, totally unrelated stuff.

Regardless, I'm guessing that your mind did NOT focus on the here and now. In other words, you probably didn't live fully in the moment for that minute or two. (That's normal.)

Here's the difference: With meditation, you seek to bring your mind to the present moment. You live in the here and now, always gently refocusing your mind when you start thinking about the past or the future.

As I mentioned in the beginning of this book, there is only ONE moment – this one. The moment you're living right now. The past is over, the future hasn't arrived... so all you have is this moment.

Now if you're struggling to keep your mind focused during meditation, perhaps all you need to do is strengthen your "focus muscle" at other times of the day. Just as a NFL football player lifts weights so he's strong on game day, you may want to practice focus and living in the now to enhance your meditation sessions.

Here's how...

Several times throughout the day, stop and pay full attention to what's going on around you. You can take inventory of what all your five senses are experiencing at the moment (as described in the Yoni Mudra section of this book). That is, you can pay attention to what you see, hear, taste, smell and touch. Alternatively, you can spend a few minutes focusing on just one sense at a time.

For example, you may focus on your touch sensation. Since you have so many touch sensations coming in constantly (most of which you regularly ignore), it may be easier to do this exercise via a body scan.

> *Note: since this isn't a regular meditation session but rather an exercise to help you sharpen your*

focus and pay attention to the present moment, you can do this any time, any place – even when you're at work or sitting in a doctor's waiting room.

Also, because this isn't a full-blown meditation session, you can do this even when you don't have much time. For example, you can do it in as little as a minute or two.

If you do a quick body scan, start at your feet and work your way up. Pay attention to how your feet feel, especially those contact points where your feet touch your shoes or touch the floor.

Go to ankles and calves. Pay attention to how the back of your calves feel where they come in contact with the chair. Take note of how your pants feel on your legs. If you're wearing shorts, a skirt or some other clothing that leaves your legs exposed, take note of how your exposed skin feels. Is it cold? Warm? Dry? Wet?

And so on. Keep moving up your body, paying attention to all the body sensations, pressure points, warmth, cold, itchy spots, painful spots and so on. Pay attention to things you usually ignore, like how your hair tickles your face or how your waistband presses into your stomach. If you're resting one part of your body on another – such as your hand on your belly – pay attention to what your hand feels, and then switch focus to the touch sensations coming from your belly.

> *TIP: You can stop and pay attention to the present moment at least five different times during the day (not counting your meditation sessions). That way you can pay attention to a different sense every*

time. In other words, rotate through your senses all through the day.

Reflect

You've just discovered why it's perfectly natural for your mind to have the tendency to wander during your meditation sessions. With practice you'll learn to maintain longer periods of focus. And you can practice even when you're not meditating, such as when you stop and focus on the present moment.

If you practice this simple focus exercise multiple times per day, soon you'll become more accustomed to naturally paying attention to the moment. And when you learn how to do that, both your every day moments as well as your meditation sessions will become much more enjoyable.

Now let's turn our attention to two other important issues. Namely, working unexpected sensations and feelings during meditation...

Handling Unexpected Body Sensations and Other Feelings

It's not unusual to experience unexpected body sensations or even unexpected (emotional) feelings during meditation.

We'll talk about both of these in this section...

Dealing with Unexpected Body Sensations

When your mind is calm and you're fully focused on the present moment, you're bound to become aware of body sensations that you've never felt before.

Indeed, if you completed the touch awareness/focus exercise

in the last chapter, then you know that your brain processes (but ignores) dozens of sensations at any given moment. For example, you habitually ignore the feel of your clothing on your skin or the pressure of your back leaning against the chair.

The only times you tend to notice these sensations are when there's something unusual about them. If your clothes are wet, you'll notice. If you're wearing shorts and sit down on a metal folding chair on a cold day, you'll quickly notice the cool metal against your skin. And the same goes for your other senses.

When you're meditating, you're more likely to notice all sensations. You'll also quickly discover that certain sensations are enhanced, only because your mind is calm and quiet enough to full appreciate the sensation. For example, you may become even more aware of any pains you have, such as a toothache. Indeed, the perception of pain is likely to be enhanced because you're more aware of it.

Handling Pain

If you begin to feel pain during your meditation session, the first thing to do is figure out if this pain is simply a result of you sitting, standing or lying in an uncomfortable position. Obviously, if you discover your position is the problem, then shift into a new position. Meditation shouldn't be an intentionally painful experience.

Now if you discover if you have a source of pain that can't be alleviated simply by shifting positions, there are two main ways for you to handle this:

- Allow yourself to casually observe the

pain, just as you would observe any other thoughts with casual detachment. You don't need to dwell on it. Just acknowledge it and move on. You may find that by returning your focus to your meditation session, the pain naturally goes away by itself.

- The second way to handle pain during meditation is to do a meditation with the intention of alleviating the pain.

  While there are a few different ways to do this, one common way is to start with a simple breathing meditation to relax you. Then you can focus on the concept of a white, healing energy swirling around your body, washing over you. Focus on this energy until you can actually begin to feel it in the room with you.

You may imagine the healing light washing over this spot like waves gently lapping on the ocean's shore. Or you may instead choose to imagine being enveloped in the energy, like you're getting an energy hug. Or yet another alternative is to focus on this light energy beaming down on your painful spot like a healing laser.

Handling Other Sensations During (and After) Meditation

It's quite common to feel other non-pain sensations rise up both during and after meditation. Some of them are just regular physical functions of the body, while others are sensations you may be quite surprised to experience.

TIP: Below I'll describe a wide range of experiences you may or may not experience. If you don't experience any of them, don't worry – that too is normal. Different individuals tend to have different experiences. In addition, different types of meditation (and different levels) also produce different experiences.

In addition, don't try to create these "energy type" sensations. If you experience them once and then try to recreate them, your mind will be focused on searching for signs that the sensation is returning. And if you're focused on this rather than on your intended object of focus, your mind is not still. As such, you're even less likely to experience the sensation again.

Physical Sensations

The first sensations we'll talk about are those regular physical sensations. For example, you may become very aware of slight twitches, movements and other sensations in your body. You may feel a muscle twitch. A finger may involuntarily move. You may become very aware of your heartbeat in different parts of your body (in your chest, your wrist, your neck, etc), and the sound of your blood rushing through your veins.

If you'd like, you can casually observe these sensations and then refocus your mind back to your mantra, your breathing or other intended object of focus.

Alternatively, you can go ahead and fully experience these sensations. For example, you may want to be mindful of how your heart beats and pumps blood all through your body. You can do a concept meditation as you think about this process. Or you may want to focus on the sound/sensation of your heart beating, perhaps even counting your heartbeats.

Another common sensation you may experience is that you become more visually aware. Suddenly you may see little dots and squiggly, transparent lines "floating" in your field of vision. When you blink or move your eyes, you see these dots and lines scurry away... but you'll likely see them (or others) float back in.

You're not imaging these "floaters" – they're real. What you're seeing are dead cells or other debris floating on your eye, right in your line of vision. Most people have these, but we've generally trained ourselves to ignore them.

Side Note: Take a moment right now to look out into the distance without really focusing on anything. Allow yourself to become aware of the movement of these floaters. Do you see them?

If you spend a minute or two becoming consciously aware of the floaters, you're likely to have a hard time getting rid of them once you turn your attention back to this book.

It's like telling someone, "don't think of a pink elephant." If you tell them that, then that's all they can think about. Likewise, sometimes when you start noticing these floaters, then you notice them almost constantly, simply because you're thinking about them. But you can't tell yourself to "stop thinking about the floaters," because that will make you even more aware of them.

Make sense? ☺

Another common physical experience is to different levels of sensory perception across all five senses. I've included some of the common perceptions below along with other physical experiences:

- *Noticeable (but temporary) changes in vision*. You may notice increased visual acuity, where everything seems so clear and bright. You're likely to notice that colors are sharper and brighter. You may even notice things "brightening" when your eyes are closed during your meditation. It may seem as if the sun is starting to shine into your eyes (even if you're sitting in a darkened room).

On the flip side, some people temporarily experience a loss of visual acuity, especially after a meditation session. You may feel like things are a little blurry and out of focus.

- *Noticeable (temporary) changes to your hearing.* Just as with vision, this can go either way. You may feel like sounds are a little louder and sharper, as if you're wearing a hearing aid that's sharpened your auditory acuity.

Alternatively, you may feel that your hearing isn't quite as sharp just after meditation session. Your ears may "ring" or you may hear an ocean sound (which is usually just you being aware of the blood rushing through your veins).

- *Noticeable tactile sensations.* We've already covered the possibility of you feeling pain and other sensations during meditation. You may feel others that we haven't talked about, such as a heightened awareness of the temperature or the slightest breeze moving around you. You may also feel tingling sensations (although you should check to make sure these sensations aren't because a part of your body is falling asleep).

- *Noticeable taste and smell sensations.* Finally, just as with the other senses in your body, your sense of taste and smell may be heightened or it may temporarily diminish. You may even taste or smell things you've never tasted or smelled before.

    TIP: Your sense of smell is tightly

linked to your emotional memories. Think about your own experiences and you'll see it's true.

For example, think of what your grandmother's house smelled like. Think about the smell of your first car. Think about the smell of those lazy summer days at the beach when you were a child.

Did you see what happened? Just thinking about those scents allowed you to almost smell them again. And as you recalled these scents, you recalled the emotions surrounding them. Perhaps you felt the love of your grandmothers, your excitement surrounding your first car, and the freedom of those summer days.

The reason I mention this here is because you may become aware of a scent during meditation... and suddenly you'll have an emotional reaction. You could be perfectly focused on your meditation and suddenly be overwhelmed by that emotion. That's perfectly normal, and we'll talk about these sorts of unexpected feelings more in the next chapter.

- *Feeling "spaced out" after meditation.* Some people report feeling unfocused and spaced out after meditation, which makes it difficult to concentrate on certain tasks. If you find this happens to you, be sure not to schedule any mentally taxing tasks right after your meditation session.

- *Feeling like you're falling or flying.* You've probably had the experience of feeling like you're falling just as you're drifting off to sleep, followed by the sometimes violent jerk of your body as you react to this sensation. Because meditation puts you in similar altered state of consciousness, it's not uncommon to feel like you're falling (or even flying). The difference, however, is that you don't have to react to the sensation – which means your body won't jerk.

> *Side Note: While this feeling is most commonly experienced during the actual meditation session, some people experience it between sessions. Please also note that this could be an energy sensation, which we'll talk about in the next section.*

- *Feeling strong, powerful and energized.* You may get a sense of these feelings during your meditation, but these feelings tend to linger. You may feel energized and powerful, like you could throw on a pair of shoes and run a marathon. You may feel like you're on a "natural high," similar to the high you get after intense physical activity (AKA the "runner's high"). As such, if you meditate right before bed and you get these feelings, you're likely to find it difficult to fall and stay asleep.

This list is not exhaustive. As I mentioned before, different people experience different sensations. You may experience things that I've never experienced or even heard about before. If you have any questions or concerns about the physical sensations in your body, please don't hesitate to email me at help@yourbestmeditation.com.

"Energy" Sensations

Most of the sensations in the list above referred to specific physical sensations. However, even though I'm going to talk about physical sensations in this section too, I'm separating them from the more "raw" physical sensations. That's because the following sensations are really "energy" sensations that masquerade as physical sensations (as that's one way for you to perceive them).

For example...

You may become aware of the blood pumping through your

body. This is a physical sensation. On the other hand, you may experience an energy sensation, such as a tingling or even vibrating sensation in the body. Perhaps you'll even feel as if energy is rising up in you and racing around your body.

These sensations may catch you by surprise, especially if you've never experienced anything like them before. Here are a few of the more common experiences:

- *Chakra sensations.* Earlier we talked about your seven chakras (energy wheels), including the crown, third eye, throat, heart, solar plexus, sacral and base chakra. As you meditate (and sometimes even after your meditation sessions end), you may experience unusual sensations at these points. You may be particularly aware of those sensations coming from your crown chakra, heard chakra or the sacral chakra.

Certain types of meditation are more likely to make you more aware of the energy moving in specific chakras. For example, because the crown chakra is tightly linked to our spiritual nature – and because meditation can bring us spiritual insight – it's common for people to experience sensations near the crown chakra (head).

The most common experiences include feeling a tingling, numbing or vibration in the head. Some people report feeling the head "opening up" (perhaps as a result of the crown chakra opening to let the energy flow more freely). Some people feel like there's water being poured onto their head. Still others get the distinct sense like their heads are being pulled upward, or they may even feel a little light headed.

While it's common to feel these sensations coming from the head, you may feel them elsewhere. For example, you may feel your pelvis opening up or it may feel tingly, vibrating or otherwise full of energy. This is your sacral chakra opening up and/or you becoming aware of the energy in that spot on your body.

- *Rushing energy sensations.* The chakra sensations are those sensations you feel on a very specific point on your body that coordinates with your chakras. However, you may also experience an overall rush of energy.

This experience may feel invigorating as it rushes all over you. For example, you may feel energy rising up out of your stomach and radiating to all points of your body. It may feel like it's coursing through you right alongside the blood in your veins. When it reaches certain points (such as the tips of your fingers), you may feel a tingling or vibrating sensation.

- *Sensations of gentle energy washing over you.* Instead of feeling an invigorating rush of energy, you may instead feel a gentle energy washing over you slowly. You may even feel as if you're soaking in a bathtub full of comforting energy.

- *Hot flashes or cold sensations.* While it's likely that you'll experience energy in terms of tingling, vibrating, rushing or washing over you, you may also experience it as a hot flash or "cold flash." This isn't a physical sensation as a result of the temperature in the room, but rather a result of you becoming aware of energy moving in your body.

- *Seeing the energy.* Sometimes if your eyes are open during your meditation session, you'll actually see the energy on you, around you and in the room. Like everything else, different individuals tend to have different experiences.

For example, you may see colors swirling around you like leaves on a breezy autumn day. Or you may instead see white or yellow lights swirling, darting, flying and dancing around you and the room.

You may even see these lights, colors and other remnants of energy even as your eyes remain closed. As mentioned previously, sometimes it can feel like the room is brightening – despite the fact that you're sitting in a darkened room with your eyes shut. This is likely due to you becoming aware of the energy that's around you.

- *Sensing the energy.* This one is difficult to explain, but you'll know exactly what I mean the moment it happens to you. Basically, you'll perceive energy in some way – but you're not actually using your physical senses to perceive it. (Some of the other sensations we've talked about may actually be experienced this way, even though they definitely feel like physical sensations.)

For example, you may be very aware of colored energy swirling around you. However, you'll realize that you're not actually perceiving these colors with your physical eyes. That doesn't mean the energy doesn't exist – rather, you're perceiving it on an intuition or spiritual level that scientists struggle to explain.

Again, this list is not exhaustive. You may experience things others have never experienced or even heard of. As usual, contact me if you have any questions or concerns about the sensations you're experiencing.

Now let's look at what sorts of unexpected feelings you may encounter...

Dealing With Unexpected Feelings

You've just discovered what sorts of physical or energy sensations you may experience during meditation. Now let's look at what sort of unexpected emotional feelings may rise up during meditation (and sometimes after).

Just as you can experience both pleasant and unpleasant physical feelings, you can experience both pleasant and unpleasant emotional feelings. Let's examine these separately...

Handling Unpleasant Feelings

Generally, meditation leaves you feeling good physically, emotionally and spiritually. So you may be surprised to find out that meditation sometimes brings up unexpected emotions.

Here's why...

When your mind is calm, it's easy for you to remember some of the thoughts and feelings that you've "stuffed away" over the years. Suddenly you can remember those who've hurt you and those you've hurt. Your sadness, anger, jealousy, greed, regret and other negative emotions rise up and become painfully obvious in much the same way that your physical pain can become enhanced.

Just as physical pain serves as a beacon to let you know about an injury in your body, emotional pain sheds light on situations where you've perceived injustice and hurt. But since humans often try to hide our negative emotions, we never fully process the situation that caused the emotion.

Most of hate when we feel jealous or angry. So when we feel that way, we automatically push it aside and tell ourselves that those are petty emotions that we shouldn't be feeling (thus adding a dash of guilt for even feeling that way). While it's true that you don't want to walk around with an angry or jealous heart, sometimes you do feel that way. But instead of pushing the feelings aside, you should examine them and then deal with them.

For example, let's suppose you feel a touch of jealousy when you hear about friend who's just finished writing a book. Guilt sweeps over you for feeling that way and you shove your jealousy aside so you can be happy for your friend.

But here's the thing: Shoving the negative emotion aside only buried it. You didn't release it. And these sorts of emotions build up over time and sometimes come bubbling up when you're sitting quietly for a meditation session.

In just a moment I'll tell you how to deal with these unexpected feelings. But first, let me say this: From here on out, you need to start processing your negative emotions when they happen. That way, you won't bury and repress them. When you bury them, all you're doing is "kicking the can down the road" – in other words, you'll just have to deal with them at some point in the future.

From now on I want you to acknowledge times when you feel angry, hurt, jealous, etc. Now ask yourself why? If you're feeling jealous and even a little angry, perhaps it's because someone is doing something that YOU want to do.

Go back to the example of your friend who's just written a book. You feel jealous. Maybe you've always wanted to write a book... and you're angry because your friend beat you to it. So you lash out at your friend.

But in reality, you're upset with yourself. You're upset because you never followed your dream of writing a book. Something held you back. Something made you scared. And all your hesitation means that years later it still wasn't finished... and your friend beat you to it.

Now you're getting at the root of this anger. In order to fully process this emotion and the situation, you'll need to acknowledge that something held you back (perhaps a fear of failure). And then you need to fix it by overcoming your fear and finally starting to take steps on your path to writing your own book.

See how that works?

Now you need to take it one step further...

Opening Your Heart to Unconditional Love and Forgiveness

While meditation can bring up an unexpected unpleasant emotion, most people who meditate develop their ability to unconditionally love and forgive. And that's important, because unconditional love and forgiveness is needed both in dealing with negative emotions as well as helping to prevent these emotions in the future.

You've probably heard the saying (which is part of a song), "All you need is love."

Typically we associate love with romantic love, the love between friends or even the love between parents and their children. In other words, we think of an emotional feeling (one that we feel whether we want to or not).

However, there is another type of love: Unconditional love. This is the love that we CHOOSE. This is when we offer love to someone without strings and without judgments. We don't judge someone based on their actions, such as by saying the person who does "bad" things is a "bad" person.

Instead, we view ourselves and those around us without judgment. We accept and love ourselves and those around us. We forgive and offer compassion to ourselves and those around us. And we do this because we are all here for different reasons, which is why we can't judge someone else's behavior as right or wrong.

Let me give you an example...

Suppose you hear about a guy who's caught stealing. Is he "bad?"

Now what if you found out that he was stealing food or medicine for his dying child? And since he didn't have money or job, this was the only way to save his child. How would you feel knowing those details?

Chances are, most people would view him much more compassionately if they knew he was stealing to save his child. People would probably instantly forgive the thief and beg the judge to let him go (and then they'd raise money to help his child).

The point is, we don't know why people do the things they do, and it's not for us to judge. Our job is to extend love, forgiveness and compassion without strings. Our job is to see the good in ourselves and others.

The reason I'm telling you all of this is because most of our hurts come as a result of being conditional (rather than unconditional) with ourselves and others. That is, we expect people to behave in certain ways. And when they fall short of our expectations, we're angry and hurt.

Notice I keep using the word "ourselves." That's because we feel guilt, regret, anger and similar emotions because we're not loving ourselves unconditionally. We set up expectations for ourselves – and we get angry when we fail to meet those expectations.

Go back once again to the example of you getting angry

because a friend finished writing the book that you wanted to write. That emotion isn't really directed at the friend. Instead, it bubbled up because you were being conditional with yourself.

You set up expectations about writing a book and you couldn't forgive yourself for not getting it done. The friend who finished his book first was just a reminder of how you disappointed yourself.

See what I mean?

You can also start seeing why love is, indeed, all you need. If you can extend unconditional love and forgiveness to yourselves and others, you will escape much of the anger, disappointment and hurt that most people carry around constantly. And it's only by clearing away the hurts of the past that you can TRULY live in the moment.

Now let's talk about how to start processing the negative emotions during meditation...

Love and Forgiveness Meditation

There are many different ways to work on love and forgiveness during meditation. What you ultimately choose depends in part on your spiritual orientation. In addition, you may choose to use a guided meditation as opposed to self meditation.

Here's just one variation of the many approaches you can use to release painful emotions and replace them with love and forgiveness...

> *Note: You need to love and forgive yourself as well as others! In the example below you'll discover how to open your heart during meditation so that you can unconditionally love and*

forgive someone else. But if you've hurt others, then you'll need to ask for their forgiveness while also extending forgiveness and unconditional to yourself.

Start by doing your usual meditation ritual, such as getting into your comfortable clothing and selecting a comfortable position. Then relax and calm your mind and body by doing a simple breath meditation (or your favorite variation) for about five minutes or so.

Now focus on your heart for a few minutes. Think of a loving energy rising up inside you, making your heart feel full. Imagine your heart opening like a large, blossoming flower. Let your love and compassion swirl all around you. Imagine that it is mixing with all the compassionate, loving and forgiving energy in the Universe.

TIP: If you're a spiritual person, then think about your god's love and how powerful, compassionate, forgiving and unconditional it is. Let that love fill you until you can physically feel it. You may just "know" it. You may actually feel it in your gut or around your heart (or even your head, the crown chakra). Or you may feel the love energy coursing through your body and washing over you.

When you feel full of love, then imagine the person you want to forgive (or the one you hurt who you want to apologize for). See the loving energy swirling around this person. Imagine a cord of light reaching out and connecting the two of you (especially your hearts).

Say what you want to say to this person. If you feel hurt by something this person did, tell him you forgive him. Then acknowledge the pain and hurt you may have caused, and in turn ask for forgiveness. Then focus on wrapping both of you in the loving, forgiving energy that's swirling around you.

At this point, you may also want to focus on releasing all the negative energy and emotions you may still be harboring. On each inhale, imagine pulling in a light or blue healing light. On each exhale, imagine expelling negative energy. Watch it come out you like a cloud – release it and watch it float away.

Dealing With Other Unexpected Feelings

Working on opening your heart to love, forgiveness and compassion should help you deal with the vast majority of unpleasant emotions. But before we leave this topic, I want to touch on one other unexpected feeling: Tension or nervousness.

You'd expect that if you're meditating, you should feel calm and relaxed. And so it takes many people by surprise when they initially feel nervous, anxious or otherwise tense when they're meditating.

Why does this happen to those who are just learning to meditate? It goes back to something we touched on earlier in the book. Specifically: Because you may not be used to truly relaxing, you may start to feel tense or anxious simply because you're not used to it. In addition, you may be reacting to the fact that you're treading into the unknown.

Let's look at these two issues separately:

- ***Tension because you're not used to relaxing***. Our society tends to reward those who work hard, while viewing others as lazy. As such, we're used to working hard. We run from one task to a next. And even at times when we're supposedly relaxing, we tend to multi-task. For example, it's not uncommon for people to do things like fold laundry while they watch TV.

When you start meditating, it's going to feel very different from most anything you've done. There is no multi-tasking. There is no thinking about what you need to do next. There is no letting your mind race at a hundred miles an hour so you can organize, plan, multi-task and work.

So what happens? You may actually end up feeling tense during meditation. You feel like you SHOULD be doing something. You feel like you should multi-task, plan and organize. You may even feel a little guilty for just sitting quietly and taking time for yourself.

Realize that this feeling may come up. If it does, acknowledge it and let it go. With practice, you'll better learn how to truly relax your mind and your body.

- ***Tension because you're treading into unfamiliar territory.*** Another common reason you may feel tense during meditation is because you're not sure what to expect. Maybe you even still hold some of the myths we talked about in the beginning of the book. Or maybe you're afraid of what you might discover in the depths of your mind if you let your subconscious thoughts rise to the surface.

These are fairly common fears. You see, we humans like to remain in familiar territory, because familiarity = safety. Let me give you an example...

Think of familiar road near where you live that may be considered unsafe by others. For example, perhaps it's a mountain road with missing guardrails and a steep decline. Or maybe it's a road with blind crossings or blind curves. Or perhaps this road has any other number of dangers, such as dangerous ruts or a dense deer population.

Here's the thing: Despite the danger on this road, if you drive it often, you probably feel very comfortable traveling it. That's because familiarity is linked to safety.

Now think of other roads you've driven when you were on

vacation or when you were otherwise traveling to places you've never been before. They could be the safest roads in your entire country. And yet you probably felt a little tense traveling them.

That's because you didn't know what to expect. You didn't know what problems might lurk around the corner, such as ice, rain, snow, mudslides, rockslides, wildlife, heavy traffic, blind crossings, steep and curvy roads, gravel rather than pavement… and so on. Even if you were told these roads were safe, you probably still felt tense.

Now think about the two different roads.

Which one would you rather travel? Chances are, you'd prefer to travel on the familiar road, simply because you KNOW what to expect.

And likewise, people who're just beginning to meditate may feel anxious simply because they don't know what to expect during their meditation sessions. Sometimes they'll stop meditating, because it's easier to stay on the familiar yet dangerous road – the one where people remain stressed out – as opposed to taking a better yet unfamiliar road (meditation).

What you need to do is acknowledge and deal with these feelings if

they rise up. Know that
with practice, you'll
become more familiar
with meditation. And as
you become more
familiar – plus as you
start experiencing all
the benefits – you'll
start feeling safer.

Now let's look at some of the
pleasant (yet unexpected)
feelings you may experience
during and between your
meditation sessions…

Enjoying Pleasant Feelings

Even though you already know
that regular meditation will make
you feel good physically,
emotionally and spiritually, you
might still be surprised by some
of the emotions that bubble up
during and between your
meditation sessions. Even if
you're not particularly surprised
by the feeling itself, you may be

surprised by the intensity and depth of the emotion.

Let's look at some of the more common feeling you may experience:

- ***Feelings of overwhelming love.*** Sometimes during meditation you may experience intense, even overwhelming, feelings of love. This tends to happen even more so when you do certain meditations (such as those where you open your heart for love), or if you do meditation for spiritual purposes.

    In addition to feeling like your heart is bursting with love for others, you may also experience the intense feeling of being loved.

You may be tapping into the Universal consciousness and/or perhaps you're becoming aware of a love from a higher power.

- ***A feeling of being connected with everyone and everything.***
Sometimes when you meditate you start to realize that everyone and everything is connected. When you love someone else, you are loving yourself and all others. When you hurt someone else, you are hurting yourself and all others.

As you develop this feeling of connection, the old political, racial, ethnic and other manmade boundaries fall away. You'll feel that the people in downtown London are just as important (and equal) to the bushmen in Africa. Those with different religious backgrounds, skin color, political beliefs and other differences no longer matter, because you'll start to focus on your similarities rather than your differences.

You'll feel connected to nature, too. You'll see how you fit into the greater Universe. You'll feel connected to the wildlife. Your new understanding may even bring about behavioral changes in you, such as you choosing to become a vegetarian.

- ***Feeling closer to your god (something greater than yourself).*** Buddhist monks have long known that meditation can be used as a direct communication line to your god (or gods). You may feel filled with Spirit and love. In quiet moments you may come to an understanding of what you are here for and what you are supposed to do. You grow in confidence as you start to understand what path you are to walk in life.

  Perhaps it's not surprising for those who use meditation primarily for spiritual purposes to feel that they are closer to their god. After all, that's why they chose to meditate. (Although sometimes the intensity of the experience can pleasantly surprise you.)

However, even those who do not use it for spiritual reasons sometimes report feeling connected to something greater than themselves. They may have a spiritual awakening of sorts – and that can be surprising, since they never started to meditate with that goal in mind.

- ***Intense feelings of euphoria / happiness / contentment.*** Many people look for happiness to occur at some point in the future, usually after some specific event happens. For example, "I'll be happy when I have more money." Or, "I'll be happy when I find a life partner." Or, "I'll be happy when I retire."

The problem is, those points of happiness are usually moving targets. Just when the person almost reaches the designated point, they redefine their happiness in terms of some other vague point in the future.

Alternatively, when the designated event happens (e.g., they retire) and they find that they still are not happy, they look for something else that will make them happy.

But here's the thing: Happiness doesn't come from outside. Other people can't make us happy. Money, objects, possessions, things... none of that can make us happy. Happiness must come from within.

Once you start meditating – once you start fully focusing on the moment – you may realize that those moments are some of the happiest moments you've ever experienced. You'll realize that happiness isn't something you strive for... rather, happiness is something that exists right now, and it can be yours if you CHOOSE it. Meditation helps you make that choice because you're living fully in the present moment and looking within for all that you need.

Reflect

The feelings I mentioned in this chapter shouldn't be considered to be an exhaustive list. For example, you may experience an intensely pleasurable feeling that's not even describable using mere words.

Now before we leave this topic, let me offer one last piece of advice: Don't try to recreate the pleasant experiences you have during your meditation sessions.

The reason is simple. If you are seeking to recreate a previous sensation, feeling or other experience, then you are not focusing on your meditation. You are thinking about the past (e.g., the pleasurable feelings you experienced previously) or you're thinking about the past (the feelings you'd like to experience again very soon). Neither are conducive to living in the moment or quieting your mind.

In short: The less you time you spend thinking about how to recreate those pleasurable feelings, the more likely it is that you WILL enjoy them again soon.

Now let's switch gears and focus on how you can start incorporating meditation in your everyday life...

Incorporating Meditation Into Your Everyday Life

In this section we'll tackle two issues:

1. How to fit meditation into your life.
2. How to choose a practice that suits you.

Fitting Meditation Into Your Life

We touched on this topic earlier in the book, such as when you learned various ways to motivate yourself to meditate (such as keeping a journal, holding yourself accountable, finding someone else to hold you accountable, etc). Now let's delve in just a bit deeper…

Some people literally have all day to meditate (if they want to). Maybe they're retired, so they can easily fit meditation into their schedule. Or perhaps you know people who seem to have a lot of free time on their hands because they have very few responsibilities. And then there are people who've devoted themselves to their spiritual practices, so their days actually revolve around their meditation sessions.

Maybe you're thinking, "Those people have it SO EASY!" And then you think about your job, your family, your social life, your responsibilities and everything else that eats up every minute of every day.

But here's the thing: There are people who are much busier than you who find time to schedule in at least a few minutes of meditation every day. You see, it's easier to find time when meditation is a priority.

Let me give you an example…

Let's suppose that I tell you I'll give you a million dollars in cash if you call me up every day for a month and chat with me for 15 minutes. Would you be able to find 15 minutes every day to do that?

You bet you would! And that's because you'd make it a priority in your life. Maybe you'd get up a little earlier in the morning just to make that call. Maybe you'd call me on your lunch break. Maybe you'd drop a lesser-priority task in your life so that you could make time for that call.

Likewise, you can do the same for your meditation – but you need to make it a priority. You may need to shuffle around your schedule, get up earlier, go to bed a few minutes later, ask someone to watch the kids sometimes, say no to the demands of others that impinge on your time and so on. But the point is, when you make it a priority, you <u>will</u> find the time.

You might need to get a little creative. Perhaps you'll have to meditate at the library, at a park or even in your car if things are little too hectic at home. Perhaps you'll have to ask your neighbor to watch your kids for 30 minutes so you can meditate – and in exchange, you then watch her kids for 30 minutes. You may have to drop another activity – like watching the nightly news – and instead get your news from the radio on the way to work.

Get creative and you'll find the time. And keep these tips in mind:

- *Consider doing activity meditation.* I mentioned before that you shouldn't really give into your desire to multi-task. However, there's nothing wrong with occasionally multi-tasking by throwing in a few sessions of activity meditation. For example, you can do a walking meditation when you exercise or even when you're walking to work.

- *Be specific and schedule ahead of time.* Ideally, you should make a weekly schedule where you write down exactly what time you'll meditate during each day of the week. If you're not specific about the time, it's too easy to end up skipping a session entirely (as you keep thinking you'll do it "later," and soon you're exhausted and it's time to go to bed).

- *Do short sessions rather than skipping meditation altogether.* Something is better than nothing. That means if something else in your life unexpectedly runs late, don't skip your meditation session.

Think of it this way...

Imagine you had to stay late at work, so that by the time you got home, you only had a few minutes before you had to hop in the car to attend an important meeting. You're starving. But since you got home late, you don't have time to fix dinner.

Do you skip dinner?

Of course not! You may not have time to fix a gourmet meal, but that doesn't stop you from eating *something* ... even if it is just a quick bowl of cereal or a peanut butter sandwich.
Likewise, even if you scheduled 30 minutes for your meditation session but you end up only having five minutes to do it, use those minutes wisely. Just as it's better to eat something than nothing, it's better to do a few minutes of meditation rather than no minutes. Doing so will make sure that daily meditation becomes a high-priority activity (and a habit).

Best of all: Once you start meditating regularly, you'll find that you become more efficient and productive. That's because you're handling your stress better. And you also have improved focus and concentration at work and at home. End result: You'll actually find that you have MORE free time!

> *TIP: Just a reminder of something I mentioned earlier: Schedule your meditation sessions like you'd schedule anything else in life. Put it on your calendar, give it a high priority, and let everyone else in your household know that this block of time cannot be changed to accommodate other activities.*

Choosing a Practice That Suits You

We've talked about the many approaches you can take when you start meditating. For example, you can do a structured (concentration) meditation or an unstructured (mindfulness) meditation session. Within those categories, you can choose from among hundreds of meditation techniques (you discovered more than a dozen in this book alone). And from there you have yet another choice, whether you want to do guided meditation or self meditation.

All of these choices bring up the question: Which ones are right for you?

Let's go over two of the main issues separately…

Structured vs. Unstructured?

Your first decision is whether you should try structured (concentration) meditation, where you focus on something like your breath, a mantra or similar... or whether you should do unstructured meditation, where you observe your thoughts and experiences without reacting to them.

Many times beginners find it easier to start with structured meditation sessions. That's because it's easier to tell if you're going off track. If you start thinking about anything besides your point of focus, then you know you need to gently acknowledge the intruding thoughts and refocus.

On the flip side, an unstructured meditation session can be more challenging for beginners. If you don't have much experience with meditation, then you may have a hard time distinguishing between "experiencing the moment" and "chasing your thoughts." And because you're not focused on any one thing, it's harder to recognize if you're chasing your thoughts.

As such, you may want to begin by doing concentration meditation sessions. Indeed, you may even start by doing simple structured meditation sessions, such as breath meditation, breath-counting meditation, body scan meditation and similar.

Once you feel comfortable with those, try out different forms of concentration meditation such as concept meditation. And once you've progressed to that level, then do give unstructured meditation a try. Experiment with all forms to find out which one is right for you.

Guided Meditation vs. Self Meditation?

Guided meditation is when you use a recording (of yourself or someone reading a script), a class, or another third-party source to lead you through a meditation session. The other alternative is to do your meditation sessions yourself without any outside help.

Which one is right for you?

Here again you should try both, as this largely a matter of personal preference. Below are just a few examples of issues that may consider:

- *Are you comfortable meditating with others?* Some people find that meditating with others (either family members, friends or perhaps even with a class) actually helps them get into the habit of meditating. In addition, they find it useful to be surrounded by others who are sharing a similar experience. If they want to talk about their meditation sessions, they know they'll have someone who understands.

Then there are those people who can't focus when they're meditating with a group. They feel a little self-conscious, afraid that maybe they're not "doing it right," and that somehow others will know if they're not doing it right.

Still others find it difficult to meditate with others because there are so many potential distractions such as people shift positions, coughing, sniffing, swallowing, sneezing, etc. Other people in the room tends to mean there are different scents in the room (from lotions and perfumes to mouthwash to body odor). And if your eyes are open, you can easily get distracted watching what others are doing.

Ask yourself honestly if you would benefit or in any way be hindered if you meditated with others. Your honest assessment will help determine whether you should consider asking a family member or friend to join you, or even if you should consider taking a guided meditation class.

- *If you use a recording, can you focus on the meditation and not on the voice*? Some people – especially those who are new to meditation – find it extremely beneficial to use guided meditation scripts and recordings.

That's because you don't have to think about what you are doing or what you need to do next as you meditate. You don't have to second guess whether you're breathing deeply enough or thinking about the right things. Instead, a guided meditation script leads you through the entire session so that you can focus 100% on your meditation.

However, some people may find the recording itself distracting.

Rather than focusing on the meditation, the listener can start focusing on the sound of the person's voice. This is especially true if you record your own meditation scripts. Because most people tend to think they "sound funny" on a recording, it's easy to get hung up critiquing the sound of one's own voice and/or how well you read the script.

As such, if you choose to do guided meditations (which I HIGHLY recommend for beginners), I suggest you use professional recordings rather than self recordings. You can choose from over four dozen different guided meditations on www.YourBestMeditation.com.

Reflect

You just discovered that there two things you need to do as you start incorporating meditation into your daily life:

1. Make time for meditation. You should schedule your meditation sessions just as you schedule other important things in your life like appointments and meetings. In addition, you need to learn to give meditation a high priority, as doing so will mean you'll always find time for it... no matter what else is going on in your busy life.

2. Choose a practice that's right for you. This takes some time and experimenting to figure out what type of meditation bests suits your needs and personal preferences. But this is an important step if you truly want to incorporate meditation into your daily life.

If you simply latch onto the first meditation technique that catches your eye, you may find that it doesn't suit you. Soon you begin to try to avoid your meditation sessions, simply because the technique you're using has turned it into a chore rather than a pleasurable activity.

Instead, spend some time finding the best methods for you. Once you do, you'll look forward to each and every session... and incorporating meditation into your daily life will be a breeze.

Now let's talk about how to use tools – and even whether you should use tools – to enhance your meditation sessions...

Enhancing Your Meditation Sessions

From time to time throughout this book I've mentioned a few tools and other ways to enhance your meditation sessions. In this chapter you'll discover even more tools to help you achieve the calm you're seeking.

But before I tell you about those products and tools, let me answer the question you probably have on your mind: Do you NEED tools in order to meditate properly?

The answer is no.

You see, meditation tools enhance the overall experience, but they are by no means necessary.

Let me give you an analogy...

You don't NEED to have air conditioning in your car. Without air conditioning, your car will still get you where you need to go. But if you have air conditioning, the entire experience is more comfortable and enjoyable. When you're sitting in air-conditioned comfort, you can focus on the journey rather than thinking about how hot and uncomfortable you are. (But you still get to your destination all the same.)

Likewise, using certain tools may not *necessarily* make you a better student of meditation – although tools like this book obviously do help – but they can make your meditation sessions more comfortable and enjoyable.

> *TIP: Sometimes the very act of gathering tools can make you more serious about incorporating meditation into your daily*

life. In other words, it helps you psychologically by firming up your commitment to incorporating meditation into your everyday life.

For example, sometimes when you start a new exercise program, you're carried forward for the first few weeks just because everything is new and exciting. You tell yourself that you'll walk "every day" – and you do, at least for a two or three weeks.

But then your enthusiasm wanes, and you start skipping your walk. So what you do is buy a new pair of walking shoes that make your walk all that much more enjoyable. And in making this purchase – even if you bought them for a low price off a clearance rack --- you essentially made a commitment to your walking program. End result: You stay on track.

The same can happen when you introduce meditation tools. It's a way of telling yourself, "I'm serious about this." And it keeps you on track.

Let's look at just a sampling of these tools and what they can do for you...

Meditation Clothing

As mentioned previously in this book, you can wear most anything you find comfortable for your meditation sessions. Just make sure it's warm enough if you find that your body temperature drops during meditation, and make sure that it truly is comfortable so that you can focus on your meditation (and not your clothing).

Also as mentioned previously, I do recommend that you purchase a comfortable outfit just for the sole purpose of meditating. That way you can incorporate changing into your special outfit as part of your meditation ritual. When you do this, you'll begin to associate the clothing itself with the calm relaxation of meditation. And that means you'll get into the right mindset even before you take your first calming breath.

Meditation Timers

Earlier in the book I also recommended that you use a meditation timer. These timers not only mark the beginning of your meditation session, they also gently mark the end of your session.

Here's why they're beneficial:

- *You can focus on your meditation rather than on the clock.* Nothing kills your focus faster than trying to keep one eye on the time so you aren't late for whatever you have to do next. A reliable meditation timer completely eliminates the need for clock-watching, so you can immerse yourself fully in your meditation.

- *They aren't distracting.* Clocks, kitchen timers and similar are distracting because of their noisy ticking off of the minutes. Even digital clocks can be distracting, especially if you're in a darkened room and the clock face is lit up or glowing.
- *They won't jar you out of your relaxing*

headspace. Finally, meditation timers are beneficial because they gently mark the end of your meditation session. They don't buzz loudly and make you jump out of your skin. As such, you'll know your session is over, but you can take a few more relaxing breaths before you turn your attention back to your daily activities.

Meditation Stools, Mats, Pillows

When we talked about positions earlier in this book, I mentioned that you can meditate in any position that you're comfortable – and that includes reclining back in your favorite chair, meditating on your bed, lying or sitting on the floor, etc.

Now if you're meditating in a chair or similar, then you probably don't need any of these tools. The exception is if you travel a lot, in which case you'll want to have some sort of mat, stool or pillow so that you can easily slip in a meditation session even when you're away from home.

If you wish to meditate on the floor or outside, or if you just want to create a special space for meditating (as part of your ritual), then you'll want to consider purchasing one of these products:

- *Meditation mat.* These mats are ideal if you do your meditation on the floor or the ground. They come in a variety of shapes, sizes, colors and materials. Chose one that you find soothing and comfortable.

- *Meditation stools, benches and chairs.* Certain meditation positions require the use of a small meditation stool (such as the seiza position). Many of these are small and thus easy to take with you almost anywhere.

- *Meditation pillow.* These come in a variety of sizes, shapes, colors and fabrics. Some of them are large and flat, and thus can be used in place of a meditation mat. The smaller ones have specific uses, such as those pillows used in place of a stool in the seiza position, or those that you sit on to ensure you're in a stable, comfortable position.

Mood-Setting and Other Meditation Tools

You can incorporate many of these mood-setting tools into your pre-meditation ritual.

For example, just lighting your candles or incense will begin the process of calming your mind and body. You may even begin to associate the scents with the calming feeling of meditation. So a quick whiff of a similar scent at the office may help calm you on a stressful day.

TIP: You don't want to overuse this technique of using your associated meditation scent to calm you in situations where you can meditate (such as at a meeting). If you start using these scents habitually in high-stress situations, you'll start to associate the scent with anxiety and tension! As such, make sure you use the scent regularly during meditation, but only RARELY at other times.

Scent-based products aren't the only way to set the mood. Some of these other tools offer visual and auditory enhancements to your meditation sessions. Here are some of my recommendations:

- *Candles, incense and other aromatherapy products.* Choose something with a light, pleasant aroma that makes you feel at peace.

- *Focus/gazing objects.* You may choose an object you already own, such as a beautiful painting, photograph or statue. You can also purchase gazing objects such as light and color videos, scrying bowls, crystals, metals and mirrors, and other soothing objects.

- *Lighting.* If you have harsh lighting in your meditation room or corner, at a minimum you may want to use a lower-watt bulb or throw a scarf over the lamp (just be sure it's not a fire hazard). You may also consider buying lamps with three-way bulbs or dimmer switches so that you can control the lighting level.

- *Music and other sounds.* You can use

music and other sounds (such as nature sounds) to help set the mood. Make sure the music or sounds are soothing, not jarring.

Guided Meditation Recordings and Scripts

As noted in the last chapter, many beginners find it easier to learn how to meditate using meditation scripts and recordings. Guided meditation allows you to fully focus on your actual meditation, as opposed to your mind straying to thoughts about what you need to do next during your meditation session.

Here are some of the guided meditations you can download at www.YourBestMeditation.com:

- Astral Projection & Travel
- Aura Viewing
- Career Advice
- Chakra Tuning
- Creativity
- Depression
- Decision Making
- Energy
- ESP/Psychic
- Flying (Fear Of)
- Happy (Waking Up)
- Health
- Hypnosis
- Intimacy
- Kundalini
- Loneliness
- Lucid Dreaming
- Manifestation
- Memory Enhancer
- Mindfulness
- Money Worries
- Motivation
- Music (Relaxation, Soothing)
- Natural Beauty
- Past Life Regression
- Peace Meditation

- Positivity & Thinking Positive
- Prosperity
- Psychic
- Regret
- Relationship Help
- Relaxation (Deep, Guided)
- Self Confidence
- Sexual Intimacy
- Sleep
- Smoking - Quit, Stop
- Spirit Guide
- Telepathy
- Water Meditation
- Weight Loss
- Yoga

Go to http://www.YourBestMeditation.com to learn more about these guided meditations.

Advanced Meditation Resources

This book has served as a good overall introduction to meditation.

However, you may decide you want to learn more about specific techniques, such as Zen meditation, concept meditation, chakra cleansing and similar. If so, then you'll need to get a book, course or even take a class on these advanced topics.

Conclusion: Taking the Next Step on Your Journey...

Congratulations – you now know how to incorporate meditation in your everyday life and enjoy all the stress-busting, heart-healthy, soothing, spiritual benefits!

Just look at what you've discovered throughout this book:

- You discovered the TRUTH about meditation as we debunked some of the most common myths.

- You found out how meditation can benefit you physically, psychologically, emotionally and spiritually.

- You learned the difference between concentration (structured) meditation and mindfulness (unstructured) meditation, plus you learned about 14 different meditation techniques that fall into these two categories.

- You found out how to control your breath, thoughts, body and your feelings like never before.

- You learned how to start incorporating simple meditation into your everyday life… starting today!

- Plus you discovered some of the very best meditation tools you can use to enhance your meditation sessions!

In short, you learned everything you need to know about practicing simple meditation!

Now I know you we went over a lot of exciting information in this book. Maybe your mind is spinning and your enthusiasm is running high! You probably have the urge to set this book aside for a few days to process all that you've learned.

That's a good idea. Then in a few days you can come back and reread all or part of this book. But in the meantime, here's what I want you to do: Get started meditating immediately.

Yes, today. Right now!

Go ahead and close this book. Then spend five minutes calming your mind. Breathe in deeply (using your diaphragm), savoring each breath. Focus your mind on your breathing, counting each breath, inhaling and exhaling as if you're enjoying the purest air you've ever experienced. When your mind wanders off the focus of your breath (and it will), gently lead it back.

OK? So close this book and give it a try right now...

Enjoy!

Made in the USA
Lexington, KY
24 October 2011